"Travis Guse has a passi
this book. His expertise
covery and strategic plai

—**BILL HARMON**, president, Southeastern
District, Lutheran Church-Missouri Synod

"Everybody wrestles to answer three questions about themselves: who am I, why am I here, and what difference am I supposed to make? In *Called 2B*, Travis Guse guides readers in a process of discovery so that, with clarity and intentionality, they can begin living out their unique calling in Christ for the good of others as a daily lifestyle. This is the fruitful and fulfilling life you are made for and saved for!"

—**GREG FINKE**, author of *Joining Jesus on His Mission*

"Travis Guse's framework for assessing vital elements of recently developed and developing methods used in contemporary coaching effectively enables readers to put into practice the methods and techniques of coaching using the underlying principles of the Christian faith. This volume will greatly benefit readers who are confronting critical questions in life and those who are called to assist others in the search for God's will in their lives."

—**ROBERT KOLB**, professor of systematic
theology emeritus, Concordia Seminary

"Travis Guse is outstanding at combining empirically tested secular strategies with biblical wisdom as he walks alongside the reader who is seeking his or her own unique calling. *Called2B* is a must-read for anyone who desires to discover and passionately live out their own authentic, God-ordained life in service to others."

—**KURT SENSKE**, author of *The CEO and the Board*

"*Called2B* is a personal and honest guidebook, packed full of practical exercises, derived from the Christian wisdom tradition. Travis Guse is the reader's sagely coach who guides individuals to discover their gifts, passions, and strengths (*DivineGPS*). As a pastor and coach, Guse in *Called2B* guides the reader to direct their *DivineGPS* into unique callings, both personal and professional, as they learn to more fully love God and their neighbor, the deepest meaning of happiness."

—**MICHAEL A. THOMAS**, president,
Concordia University Irvine

Called2B

Called2B

*How to Discover and Live Out
Your Calling in Christ*

TRAVIS GUSE

Foreword by Chad Hall

WIPF & STOCK · Eugene, Oregon

CALLED2B
How to Discover and Live Out Your Calling in Christ

Wipf & Stock
An Imprint of Wipf and Stock Publishers
199 W. 8th Ave., Suite 3
Eugene, OR 97401

www.wipfandstock.com

PAPERBACK ISBN: 979-8-3852-0821-0
HARDCOVER ISBN: 979-8-3852-0822-7
EBOOK ISBN: 979-8-3852-0823-4

VERSION NUMBER 02/20/24

I WANT TO TAKE this opportunity to dedicate this book to a few important people in my life. First, I want to thank my wife Stephanie, without whom I could not have completed this book. She did not give up on me the many times I wanted to give up on myself in this process. Her encouragement and support provided the strength I needed to see this book through to completion. The saying "Behind every great man is a great woman" is so very true when it comes to my wife. Steph, you are truly a gift from God! I also want to thank my amazing son, Kendall, who has always believed in me and has invested his many talents and gifts in support of my calling in ministry. Son, without you I could not see many of my crazy dreams and visions become a reality! Please know how very much I love and appreciate you both.

Additionally, I want to thank Dr. Robert Kolb, who has served as a mentor in my love, understanding, and application of our rich Lutheran theological tradition, especially in regards to Luther's teaching on vocation. I also want to thank Dr. Chad Hall for his friendship and mentorship for me in my growth and development as a coach. You both have shown me such generosity with your time—thank you! I also want to thank the many people, some of whom are highlighted in this book, for the opportunity to serve and walk along with you as your coach. Please know that each of you have blessed my life in countless ways.

Lastly, I want to thank Almighty God, from whom all blessings flow in Christ. You redeemed not only my life, but all my mistakes and experiences as well. Thank you for pouring your love, forgiveness, and new life into this earthen vessel, and using me for your purposes to be a blessing to others.

Contents

Foreword

THE BEST VERSION OF my life—the ultimate version of success in life—is the one that is most aligned with God's calling. This has been a hard-won lesson for me. Maybe the same is true for you.

When I was a college freshman, I felt hopelessly without direction. I knew I needed a major and that my major would prepare me for a career. But I had zero context for making these life-altering decisions. I felt like I was grocery shopping in an Asian market where I couldn't read the labels, didn't recognize the selections, and didn't know enough even to begin to make a decision.

In my season of uncertainty, God spoke clearly and compellingly. The medium through which God chose to speak still makes me smile. On a Friday afternoon in November of 1989, I read an article in *Sports Illustrated* about the Liberty University football team. As I read about how the players and coaches sought to be witnesses for Christ in a game of competition and aggression, God revealed a powerful truth to me. I admitted to myself that if all of this Jesus stuff that I'd grown up learning about and confessing were true, then it should change everything about how I lived.

The best way I can describe my life since that Friday afternoon is "oriented." Since then, I have had direction. I have known good from bad. I have been able to discern right from wrong. And I have been challenged to align my thoughts, feelings, attitudes, and actions to God's truth. Of course, I have had failures along with successes, but even my failures make the point: God revealed to me what success in this life was, and it was up to me to pursue it.

It was from a place of conviction and calling that I said yes to some things and no to some other things. I said no to a girlfriend who was unwilling to be in a chaste relationship that matched God's instructions on intimacy before marriage. I transferred schools in order to say yes to preparing for a career in church ministry. I said yes to prayer and devotion while doing my best to say no to foul language and a selfish spirit. And what I experienced in that early season of calling was freedom—a freedom that can only be experienced when one is in service to something great and good and God-centered. Over thirty years later, I still rejoice in the wonderful liberty I know as God's servant.

Each of us is pursuing a version of success. To the best we can define it, each of us has a vision of what we want from life. This vision is not always clear. Our notion of a life well lived can be murky, muddled, or even conflicted. And each of us attempts to live according to our vision of success to some degree. Sometimes we lack the motivation. Other times we lack the skills or know-how. But we make decisions, take action, and think in the direction of what we consider to be a good life. Like a Roomba vacuum hunting its way back to base, each of us half-blindly knocks about en route to our best understanding of purpose. Even when our vision for a good life is wrong, we pursue it.

You have undoubtedly noticed some people who are more tuned in, intentional, and motivated to pursue their best life. These are the people who live with purpose. They know they are created on purpose and for a purpose. They seem to be drawn forward, not to some self-defined version of success, but to a vision given to them by God. In the Christian world, we call this dynamic a "calling."

God calls each person in the same way and in ways specific to the person. God calls each and every human into a life-giving relationship with God and with one another. God calls each person to join with him in the work that he is doing in the world. And God calls each person to become the highest and best version of himself or herself—a version that is capable of living in God's very presence forever and actually liking it.

God also calls each person in ways that are distinct. The more you are tuned in to God, the more you find your vision for the good life in his truth, and the clearer and more compellingly you will hear his call. When a person is in a right relationship with God, he will reveal to that person the work he has for that person as well as the resources God has given that person to fulfill the calling. This calling brings freedom, fulfillment, and the best version of success possible.

In your hands is a book that can be used by God to give you the freedom, fulfillment, and success in life I am describing. God wants to speak to you through the words Travis has written. Through the models, frameworks, questions, exercises, examples, and descriptions Travis shares in this book, you can experience the reality of God's calling on your life, and you can join the myriad of others who know they are created on purpose and for a purpose by a God who never makes mistakes.

My prayer is that God will use this book in a mighty way in your life.

With blessings and hope,

Rev. Dr. Chad Hall, MCC
President, Coach Approach Ministries

Introduction

IF YOU'RE ANYTHING LIKE me, when I was younger, I thought I knew a great deal about myself and what life was all about. In our early days, we tend to see reality through our own perceptions and experiences. However, as I've gotten older and hopefully wiser, I have found that life is, more often than not, filled with more questions than answers. However, I have realized that there is a general truth in life: "The more I learn, the less I seem to know." And on top of this, I had experiences as I matured that challenged many of my preconceived notions. Perhaps you find yourself like me, pondering some of the profound questions of life many wrestle with:

- "Who am I?"
- "Why am I here?"
- "What is my purpose?"
- "What difference am I supposed to make?"

To add to the complexity, when searching for explanations to these monumental questions of life, we're often more likely to discover clues than find answers. Most people struggle with them for a long time. They aren't like the answers to grade school math tests in an appendix at the back of a textbook. Instead, they're contextual, layered, and influenced by the paths we take in life. They're perhaps products of relationships, upbringings, marriages, careers, and unique perspectives.

The good news is that even the most deeply grounded people never truly answer them—at least, not in every sense of the word. Or, if we do, we still have trouble accepting the reality. To quote the title of a song made famous by the band U2, many of us resonate with the feeling "I Still Haven't Found What I'm Looking For." As a result, we suddenly become our own worst critics. We'll do anything to discover a sense of our own identity by wrestling with it, avoiding it, second-guessing ourselves—anything to push the answers back into the grasp of the frustrating refrain, "I don't know."

Answering—and accepting—the answers to these questions is the quest of everyone who's ever worn the title of human being. This is simply part of this journey we call life.

To gain ground in this journey, we'll need better answers than the typical "I don't know." And if we need better answers, we've got to start by asking better questions.

Many people around you, even people making progress in some areas of life, puzzle over their purpose. Some think this question is unique to people grappling with depression or lacking direction. But I assure you, if you haven't already wondered about your identity, security, and the meaning of your life, you almost always will at some point.

That was me after I'd been in ministry for six and a half years and received my first call as a pastor after seminary. Contrary to my expectations, I struggled to find peace when I became a pastor. I found myself at odds with my work environment. Methods, decisions, and values in that particular congregational context clashed strongly with my values and ministry philosophy. It wasn't long before I found myself stuck between the proverbial rock and a hard place.

I was in a situation where my values did not match the rest of the ministry team. It was my first call as a pastor, and with fresh out of seminary enthusiasm, I was engaged and motivated to put my best foot forward in my new role. However, my ministry partner, unfortunately, did not share that same enthusiasm and might have been dealing with a good degree of burnout after years in his role. Not knowing how to navigate such a challenging work situation, especially as someone who had never experienced the feeling of burnout, I did not cope with the situation well at the time. Now, after years of ministry under my belt, I better understand burnout and its effects on your context and those around you.

Have you ever been in a situation where the thought of work fills you with dread? Our professional lives consume enormous amounts of time each week—as much as 50 percent or more of all waking hours. Perhaps you may know how it feels to despise or dread most of your waking hours.

Working as a professional church worker is no different than working in a secular job. We daily deal with people impacted by this sinful, broken world, no matter if the work environment is in the "sacred" or "secular" space (though my conviction is that all of life is holy, not just those places we call church). Sometimes, our own misguided responses to these difficult situations do not always glorify God. When I struggled in my work relationships in my first call as a pastor, I lost the sense of joy in my work and became disillusioned instead.

One thing I learned, looking back at this, is that the longer we stay in a context misaligned with our identity, values, and convictions, the more prone we are to making decisions we will regret. We start making comparisons—the thief of joy. We forget the old warning, "The grass isn't always greener on the other side." We dream of being anywhere other than where we are currently.

After a while, an opportunity to escape presented itself with another church. I was so eager to leave my current environment with all its frustrations that I leaped at it without hesitation.

Only after I'd signed on the dotted line and committed myself to accept the call to a different ministry did I realize that I may have acted out of unresolved internal frustration instead of divine direction. My "fight or flight" response was in high gear. If only I had a person walking with me at the time as a sounding board, helping me process the thoughts and feelings I was wrestling with to help me see my situation more objectively.

The new position had the opposite effect. It compounded my pain and frustration because, before long, I had to withdraw and tell the congregational leaders the bitter truth. I was running away from something rather than toward something. I accepted the call for all the wrong reasons. This decision felt like a rebound relationship—like someone who just went through a breakup and immediately rebounded by dating someone else. And it turned out the new someone needed to be a better match. It was embarrassing and discouraging.

In hindsight, after stepping away from ministry for a season, I realized that my identity had unintentionally become so wrapped up in my role as a pastor that I'd misplaced its original and authentic source—being a child of God! As a result, I felt exposed and began to scramble to hide my sense of failure.

It may come as a surprise to you, but paid professional ministry can affect a person's sense of self in ways loosely parallel to becoming a professional athlete or Hollywood celebrity. It is easy to look to the role of professional church worker (and/or one's career) for one's ultimate sense of identity. There is enormous validation in being needed and valued for what one could offer in one's role.

All it took to expose my weak foundation was a lengthy period of not being needed, sought out, or consulted. Not only had ministry taken a sour turn, but now having to step away from full-time ministry for a season seemed to sour everything else in my life in the process!

The in-between period of wandering can leave a person feeling abandoned and questioning their life's purpose. You can be sure you're in the wilderness when you start to think things like:

- "God exists . . . but he seems absent in my life."
- "He hears and answers prayer . . . but am I on his radar?"
- "He has a calling and purpose for other Christians . . . but what about me?"

Eventually, I started feeling like I was going through the motions each day but couldn't truly engage the world around me. I felt no happiness or joy. Sometimes, I didn't even feel sadness; there was only an overwhelming numbness. I had a level of energy sufficient to stay alive physically, but that was all. Spiritually, it was like being in a coma—neither dead nor alive in any meaningful sense. So I asked myself a question similar to what God asked the prophet Ezekiel when he saw the vision of the Valley of Dry Bones: "Son of man, can these dry bones live?" My response was the same as Ezekiel's, "Lord, only you know" (Ezek 37).

I couldn't see it then, but in hindsight, I realized God was deeply involved every step of the way, breaking me down so that he could build me back up again. No matter how you feel about God, you've probably experienced a season of tearing down and building back up. These are those crucible moments of life when a person gets melted down to the core of their being, only to be reforged into something better, more valuable than before. By faith, I believe there is a moment in our life when God saves us and another moment he begins to remake us (sometimes they can be one and the same). If you disagree, consider your life over the last ten years versus today. Whatever your age, things you thought, said, and did back then have changed. You're not the same person you were ten years ago.

As it turns out, we don't complete the maturity process simply by graduating from high school or college. Adulthood has more tests and unexpected challenges, not less. The stakes are higher and more consequential. And how you respond to them will influence your decisions and future well beyond the present moment.

In the midst of my wilderness experience, my eyes were suddenly opened to God's unique workmanship in my life. I came across a leadership training hosted by Mosaic Church when I lived in Southern California. As part of their leadership development process, they utilized a relatively new assessment tool at the time to equip their leaders, the StrengthsFinder® Assessment (recently rebranded by Gallup® as CliftonStrengths®). I'd never done anything like it before, but something about it clicked with me immediately when I took the assessment. I suddenly had language for things I had always sensed about myself but couldn't put into words. It clarified mysteries I'd wrestled with for years—about God's design and purpose for my life.

For many years as a pastor, I often felt like a square peg, trying to fit into a round hole in pastoral ministry. I wasn't your proto-typical "shepherd-teacher" pastor. Instead, I was future-oriented, entrepreneurial, and missional. I wanted to create and innovate rather than manage and maintain. CliftonStrengths® helped me understand how I naturally think, feel, and behave as part of God's gifting and design in my life. As an example, my top talent theme is being an Includer®. According to the CliftonStrengths® Assess-ment, connecting with people on the outside, looking in, and help-ing them feel like they belong resonates at my core.[1] Suddenly, I felt like I had permission to live that gifting out in my life—I didn't need to force myself to fit into a specific mold of service. Instead, I could be who God had created and redeemed me to be to love and serve others.

As I made these discoveries of God's workmanship in my life, I found myself wondering if I wasn't alone. What if, all along, I'd stared into the faces of hundreds of worshipers during a Sunday sermon and completely missed the opportunity to empower them to discover who God had created and redeemed them to be? What if I could have shown them how they could live out their God-given callings without fitting into some predetermined mold? What if this could happen worldwide, in churches large and small, in every denomination? How many believers are being under-served by a generic, formulaic understanding of what it looks like to serve God by serving others? What if we have a rich, satisfying, and life-giving alternative that is both biblically and theologically grounded to fall back on?

Perhaps even more important, how would it look different to impact people on a deeper, more profound level—one where they felt inspired when I share what I've learned? What could I do differ-ently to turn myself into a conduit for that to happen? Amazingly, I discovered the answer through coaching (and being coached).

While life and executive coaching, like the field of counsel-ing, were developed independently from the sphere of faith, they

---

1. Gallup®, CliftonStrengths® and the CliftonStrengths 34 Themes of Talent are trademarks of Gallup, Inc. All rights reserved.

are a helpful tool for ministry that is being utilized more and more within the church. A professional coach works with another person by guiding them through an intentional process that empowers that person being coached to make discoveries, find solutions, and move forward in taking action steps aligned with their vision and goals in living out their various callings in life. Ultimately, the coach focuses on a process that allows the coaching client to find their own solutions.

While counseling is past-oriented and typically aimed at helping those who receive it find healing, coaching instead is future-oriented and aimed at assisting relatively well-adjusted people in developing future-oriented goals and taking action. A key distinction between coaching versus other helping professions like consulting or mentoring is that the expertise lies not with the coach but with the person being coached. The coach is an expert in the coaching process, while the client is the expert of their life.

During this time of wandering and discovery, I worked with a coach named Mike Ruhl. With his listening ear and caring disposition, Mike helped me process things that weighed heavily on my heart and mind. We worked together to rebuild the foundation of my calling in life and ministry, starting with this: my true calling and identity are in Christ alone, not in what I do for a living.

When I discovered and experienced the power of coaching with Mike, I knew I wanted to help others find the same pathway to discern their callings in life better. He helped me develop a strategy to get there. In addition to providing me with personal care, his guidance empowered me to deepen my awareness of and live out my authentic calling in Christ. He took the time to help me process each potential way forward. His questions revolved around one critical focus: "Who have you been created and redeemed to be, and what is the best way to live out that calling from God in love and service to others?" That helped to eliminate several second-rate scenarios until we found the one where my only answer to Mike's big question was "Yes."

Yes, I want to help people stop struggling and start thriving by discovering who they are in Christ and how they have been gifted.

Yes, I want to help believers know why they are here in this place at this time, and for what purpose.

Yes, I want to help people know how to harness their unique Gifts, Passions, and Strengths to make a difference in the lives of others.

Yes, I want the lifestyle of a coach—getting deep in the trenches of people's lives, helping them process and grow by transcending perceived limitations to live the life God was calling them to live, to be a greater blessing to others all around them.

As Mike journeyed with me through my wilderness experience, the decisions I made due to his coaching filled me with confidence. I was not merely seeking God's will for my life but also putting it into practice. As a result, I felt even more fulfilled when I began to coach my own clients. There was no longer a mere transmission of knowledge or information in regards to helping everyday believers discover and live out their unique calling in Christ in their personal lives; now, there were concrete steps, plans, actions, and results. There was deeper awareness and more action. Isn't that what we all want in our lives? Isn't that also what God wants for us in this life—not just knowing his love and salvation in Christ but also making a more significant impact in the lives of others as we love and serve our neighbors?

Of all the stories and details I could share about my life and journey, this is by far the most compelling one because it marked a significant turning point in my life. It's a story I get to refresh and spin a hundred different ways as I work with each new coaching client. Of course, the narrative changes with each person I work with, but there are way more significant impacts than there used to be.

Moreover, I'm no longer simply writing new stories for myself every day. I also have the privilege of walking along with others as a coach, helping them author their own stories as they live their lives connected to God's grand story of life in Christ's kingdom. Eternity is the destination for everyone who trusts in Jesus by grace through faith. But in the meantime, we all have a personal path to walk through this life of calling, in love and service to others, being used by God as conduits of his provision and care to the world.

That's where I'm headed on this journey. And in the following pages that form our time together, I invite you on that journey of discovery.

Every journey has a beginning, the journey itself, and a destination. We will start this journey by helping you deepen your awareness of your *authentic identity*, shaped by your *ultimate identity* in Christ, which serves as your "true north," and your *unique identity*, of better understanding your Divine GPS (Gifts, Passions, and Strengths) to navigate your various calling in life. Next, we will explore the importance of *empowerment* so that you can practice good self-care regarding your heart, soul, mind, and body so you can show up as the best version of yourself for the sake of others. Lastly, we will conclude this journey by helping you make a greater *impact* by engaging your Divine GPS to love and serve those God has placed in your various areas of responsibility in life.

Essentially, this entire journey is your call to discipleship as summed up by Jesus in his conversation with the expert of the law, "Love the Lord your God with all your heart, and with all your soul, and with all your mind and with all your strength. The second is this, Love your neighbor as yourself." (Mark 12:30–31 NIV) The neat thing is that each of us are going to love God and love our neighbor in unique ways according our divine Gifts, Passions, and Strengths. Our life's purpose is lived out based on that truly unique workmanship and calling we each have.

Now, let's work together to discover your authentic calling in Christ!

1

One Body, Many Parts

HAVE YOU EVER PAUSED to consider your body? As strange as it sounds, the human body is an extraordinary thing. Take a moment to feel your heartbeat. Pay attention to the warmth of your skin or the way your chest lifts and lowers every time you breathe. Wiggle your fingers . . . then your toes. Feel the way every joint extends and contracts. Each intricate part of the body, all 78 organs, 206 bones, and 650 muscles, are so fragile independently, but when combined together, they create a system that is capable of doing amazing things. If you're looking for proof, look no further than Jordan Romero, the youngest person to reach the summit of Mount Everest at the age of 13 years old, or Australian swimmer Chloe McCardel, who swam the longest continuous marathon swim in history at 78 miles in 42.5 hours. With just the intricacy of our bodies it shows us evidence of endowed uniqueness as we bear the image of the Creator who made us.

Of course, you might wonder why I go to such great lengths to praise the human body. After all, we fall short in both our soul and flesh, so what makes this imagery special? It has to do with the age-old image of "the body of Christ." You know how it goes from

Paul's description in 1 Cor 12: Every body is made up of many parts, but none of those many parts do the same thing, this being a reflection of Christ's body—the church. One body, many parts.

Early in my faith journey, however, I never saw myself as an essential appendage within the body of Christ. There were those I observed that were clearly Christ's hands or some individuals who so easily reflected Christ's heart. However, in my case, if I had to be one part of this grand anatomy, I thought of myself as the belly button more than anything else—not serving a purpose, and just kind of there. But isn't that how many of us feel at some point in this journey called life, and especially in the church?

I mean, it is generally easy to see how a pastor, worship leader, or children's director is a vital part of Christ's body. Yet, I believe there is an important question we need to ask ourselves: Are pastors and ministry professionals the only active participants within the church? Are congregants, in other words, relegated to simply being passive observers of those who do active ministry on their behalf? Are they here to just pray, pay, and obey? Do we believe that a precious few are called to do God's work while the average parishioner in the pews is called only to support them with their prayers and tithes (not to say this kind of support is not important)?

Perhaps we should question whether we're being cynical and assuming too little of God's people. By doing so, do we unintentionally create "consumer Christians" who attend church primarily for what they can get out of Sunday morning? Or are they there because they want to actively participate in the overall mission of God's work in the world?

More than just discouraging everyday believers from fully living out their God-given callings, this also helps reinforce the unfortunate cultural stereotypes about the church. First, there's the perception from outsiders that it's an exclusionary club with insider cliques or a tax-exempt business interested only in social conformity and legalistic righteousness. We already have enough trouble overcoming these perceptions in our cultural climate today; the last thing we need is to worsen things by making them seem true.

Have you ever asked the question, "Is this all there is to being a follower of God?" There has to be more. It can't be just pastors and church workers who have holy callings. What sense does that make? Don't get me wrong; there is value in the service of those who answer the calling to full-time ministry. However, the truth we hear in Eph 4:11 is that Jesus called some to be pastors and other professional church workers to equip God's people for their acts of service. Callings are true and real for every believer, not just the clergy, whose calling is actually to prepare everyday believers for theirs.

You have a profound calling on your life from God. You are here in this place, at this time, for a specific purpose that God has in mind for you to experience and live. No matter what part of the body of Christ you are, you are a vital part and have a unique contribution to make, not only within the church but also as a part of the church. You are a valuable part of Christ's body, his living presence to the world around you.

When Jesus said in Luke 9:23 (NIV), "Whoever wants to be my disciple must deny themselves and take up their cross daily and follow me," did he mean what he said? Are those words for a select few, or are they for everyone who follows Jesus? God calls each believer to impact the world today, especially those closest to them. Perhaps the full and abundant life Jesus calls us to live in John 10:10 is about more than just sitting with a ticket in our hands and waiting for the glory train to come to take us to eternity (as amazing and wonderful of a gift as that is, thanks to Jesus). God has prepared a life filled with purpose for each of us to live out in our lifetime so that his will may be done here on earth as it is in heaven.

2

Discerning Your Calling

How DO WE KNOW the will of God for our lives? Imagine if God had uniquely gifted you to lead a Fortune 500 company effectively, and you resisted in favor of going on overseas mission trips in Third World countries because that seems like the "godly" thing to do. Would you be walking in obedience or disobedience?

"Well," you might say, "Christ calls us to help the poor. Working in a Fortune 500 company doesn't do that nearly as much as working in an orphanage in Cambodia."

Now, please don't hear what I am not saying. I am not saying that one shouldn't help the poor, especially if God has laid that on your heart. I'm not even saying that working at an orphanage in Cambodia may not be within God's will for your life as a follower of Jesus. However, how could you definitively know that God only calls you to work with the poor overseas and nowhere else? Nowhere in the Bible does God say, "Whatever you do, it must directly help the poor. So don't do anything that doesn't singularly help the poor in some faraway land." What if the Fortune 500 company that you work for manufactures packaging for food items that are distributed all over the world? Or what if the profits of this company are so significant that compassionate initiatives are started with some of the earnings to help feed underprivileged children around the world?

Scripture does say, "Whatever you do, do it all for the glory of God" (1 Cor 10:31 NIV). That's the criteria: Does it glorify God? If it does, how would we know? Is God only glorified when his people specifically help the poor? When Mary Magdalene, in John 12:1–8 (NIV), poured expensive oil on the Lord's feet and wiped them with her hair, Judas Iscariot was quick to criticize her on similar grounds: "Why wasn't this ointment sold," he sneered, "and the money given to the poor?" (Though secretly, Judas was skimming off the top of the ministry funds to line his own pockets and cared nothing for the poor.) But Jesus did not agree with him at all. "Leave her alone," he replied. "You will always have the poor among you, but you will not always have me."

How do we know we are glorifying God? One way to know we glorify God is by aligning our response to Christ's own words: "If you love Me, keep My commands" (John 14:15 KJV). In other words, God is glorified when his people are obedient to his will and purpose. That very well may include being charitable but not necessarily serving as an overseas missionary. If God has uniquely gifted you to make the most significant impact in loving and serving your neighbor by working among executives in a Fortune 500 company, then perhaps that's where you are meant to be. But if you went on long-term overseas mission trips instead, would you be maximizing your divine potential? Ultimately, the question we need to answer is "Where can I be the greatest blessing and do the most good with whom God has gifted and called me to be?" That might be serving overseas as a missionary, or it may be in a boardroom in a major corporation—either can bring glory to God.

In its simplest form, this is discipleship according to Luke 6:40 (NKJV), "A disciple is not above his teacher, but everyone who is perfectly trained will be like his teacher." Discipleship is simply following, obeying, and imitating Jesus in whatever you do in life. If he leads you to the corridors of corporate behemoths like Google, Apple, Microsoft, or Facebook, guess what? You go and reflect him. Your assignment details will become apparent when you get there, and you trust God knows what he's doing. You only need to focus on being a good and faithful ambassador, conducting yourself the same way as if Jesus were doing it himself.

I hope you don't need reminding—none of this applies to work God expressly forbids, such as crime, prostitution, smuggling, kidnapping, selling drugs, terrorism, assassinations, etc. You don't need to wonder if you've been "called" to be a criminal as in the hit TV show *Breaking Bad*; it's a contradiction in terms. None of these activities are within the scope of a godly calling, for they do not bring God glory and are not for the benefit of one's neighbor. We hear clearly from Jesus in John 10:10 (NIV), "The thief comes only to steal and kill and destroy; I have come that they may have life, and have it to the full." To be in God's will is to be someone who seeks to bring the abundant life that God intends to those around them.

To better understand God's will, I often use the imagery of a river. Imagine for a moment you are going on a whitewater rafting trip. When the river rafters are floating down the river, they are moving toward their destination. As with God's will, being in the river is moving according to his will. There are parts of the river that are slow-moving and other parts that flow quickly. While there may be parts of the river that have a better flow than others to get the best ride, no matter what part of the river you are currently navigating, to be in the river is to be within God's will. As you do, there is also a recognition that the river has a power and flow of its own, and it can take you where it will, no matter how hard you try to navigate. So it is with God's purpose. Outside of the river represents being outside of God's will. It's evident when you are out on the banks, you are out of the river. These are moments in which we have taken ourselves "out of the game," so to speak.

In Eph 4:1 (NIV), the apostle Paul encourages his hearers, "As a prisoner for the Lord, then, I urge you to live a life worthy of the calling you have received." To get a complete picture of this concept of "calling," I started by examining Martin Luther's teaching on vocation and its theological framework to answer these profound questions of life and faith. The word *vocation* comes from the Latin word *vocatio* (German *beruf*), meaning "to call" or "calling."

The life of vocation for believers begins when they are called by grace through faith in Christ to become a child of God (Eph 2:8–9; 1 John 3:1). In relationship to God, this ultimate identity of who we're called to be defines and sanctifies what we do in our everyday lives in relationship with those around us in our various areas of responsibility in life. Through Luther's teaching on vocation, we see through the eyes of faith that we've been gifted for specific good works, which God prepared in advance for us to do (Eph 2:10). This leads to the question: "How do we know what kind of good works we are uniquely called to do?"

Over several years of study, I formulated a theologically grounded vocational coaching framework—Called2B—to empower believers to discover and live out their authentic calling in Christ in their daily callings in life. I've refined it to the present day as I continue to help others discern their identity in Jesus and their unique calling in love and service to others.

What is the value of coaching in discovering and living out one's calling in Christ in the everyday callings in life? As Morpheus told Neo in the movie *The Matrix*, "There is a difference between knowing the path and walking the path." It is one thing to know you have a calling; however, it is another to discern and live it out. What does this look like practically?

Let's look at another example of someone living out their calling in their everyday lifework. Gina is a doctor on the pediatric floor of a large hospital, rushing from room to room. So many sick patients need medical attention, and she has worked a long day. She has dealt with worried and emotional parents, sick kids, and high expectations for her professionalism and ability to diagnose ailments correctly.

One child in particular needs her immediate attention. The nurses are pushing for the boy to be admitted because his fever is sky-high. Already weary from a long day pounding the linoleum, Gina enters an exam room with a sobbing child, his exhausted mother, and the challenge of examining and diagnosing him.

The first thing Gina encounters when she steps into the small sterile exam room is an uncomfortable, overheated little boy who doesn't want to sit still. His mother is trying to comfort him, and it is apparent she is also tired. There are bags under her eyes. She is still wearing pajamas from the night before, most likely because she was up all night with her son.

The exam is a struggle. It's hard to truly understand the child's oxygen levels or hear his heartbeat. Once Gina finally gets the correct readings, she confirms that the little boy needs to be admitted quickly. The following conversation is difficult; no parent wants to hear it, and it frequently surfaces guilt. Having your child admitted to the hospital is scary; some parents feel like they've lost control of the situation. After the day Gina has had, it would be easy to give the child's mother the facts and walk away. She could let the nurses handle the paperwork and head off to the break area for some rest.

However, Gina is no ordinary doctor. She knows that she is a physician whom the King has called. Gina is clear regarding her identity in Christ and her call to love and serve others with the best God has given to her. And despite her body's fatigue, she says a quick, silent prayer as she taps into her energy reserves. One of Gina's strengths happens to be Empathy®, which she was gifted for this divine purpose.[1] Her calling as a doctor is to help others, so she takes a different approach.

"Ma'am?" she says, sitting gently beside the mother.

The mother looks up at Gina, eyes wide, gently patting and rocking the wailing boy in her arms. "Is he okay?" she whispers.

Gina keeps her voice calm. "Ma'am, he will be okay, but your son must be admitted immediately. His oxygen is low. The nurses are going to come and help get him admitted."

It's then that it happens; you can see the mother's face crumple, and her eyes begin to water. She swallows once, twice, seeming to struggle with the words.

"I . . . I don't understand. What did I do wrong?"

---

1. Gallup®, CliftonStrengths® and the CliftonStrengths 34 Themes of Talent are trademarks of Gallup, Inc. All rights reserved.

There it is, just as expected: guilt. It weighs heavily on every parent whose child gets sick enough to go to the hospital. It's natural. Gina has seen it a thousand times at this point in her career.

A nurse comes in and gently takes the child. Then, they bring a cart to wheel him to his new room. The nurse prepares the room quickly and efficiently. Then, watching with the dread of a parent fearing for their child's life, the mother stands to follow the nurse.

"Ma'am?" Gina asks again to get the mother's attention. The mother looks at the doctor, now wiping her tears. "Ma'am, you didn't do anything wrong. You are doing a good job. His condition is not your fault."

The mother's tears flow over, and she quickly wipes them away as she nods and grasps the doctor's hand with a squeeze. She breathes a little easier. Her tense shoulders relax slightly, and she can function again. As the nurse guides her out, she follows behind her child quickly, reaching in to offer a hand for her son to hold. She looks back and gives the doctor a quick nod.

The comfort this doctor gave to that mother with those kind words made a world of difference. Nobody would have blamed Gina for stating facts and walking away, especially after a long day. But, instead, she paused and remembered her calling. When the people of God show up as they're meant to, it makes an enormous difference—especially in such a tense situation. At that moment, Gina was the blessing from God that both the little boy and his mother needed. And through the eyes of faith, as Luther taught, Gina was serving as God's mask, in a hidden way, in that moment as well. God was also loving and serving this child and his mother through Gina's calling as a doctor.

In the Lord's Prayer, as we in the church call it, Jesus taught his disciples to pray this petition: "Give us this day our daily bread." How does God give us our daily bread? While he can do so miraculously as he did with manna from heaven for his people, Israel, as they wandered in the wilderness on the way to the promised land, or as Jesus did with the feeding of the five thousand, God usually works through the callings of everyday people to give us our daily bread. He works through the farmer who grows wheat, through the miller who grinds that wheat into flour, through the baker who takes that flour and bakes bread, through the delivery truck driver who delivers that bread to the store, through the cashier who sells you that bread, and through moms and dads who make their kids PB and J sandwiches. Through each step, God works in a hidden way to bring his blessing and care in the form of daily bread to the world. And he does the same through you as you live out your calling in Christ through your various areas of responsibility in life.

I once had a member of my church who said to me, "Pastor, I want to do something significant for God." I asked him, "What do you do for a living?" He replied, "I coordinate the delivery of medical supplies worldwide for a company." I responded to him, "You are doing something significant for God—you are part of God's means of bringing health and healing around the world!"

As we consider our calling in life, "serving one's neighbor" means more than the people living next door. (Very few people do such things anyway, Christian or not. Do you know your neighbors? Bonus points if the answer is yes.) Instead, this means helping people we encounter in ways that bless and honor them wherever we meet them! The most helpful starting point is to know our God-given talents so we can activate and apply them at the right moments. Equally important, we also must know those ways we are not as gifted. Then, we can avoid getting involved in tasks where we know we lack ability, strength, or aptitude.

Coaching is a personal and practical way to begin a journey of discovery and live out who you've been created and redeemed to be in Christ. Creating awareness around who you are in Christ and God's workmanship and design in your life is the first step. We then learn to leverage these talents he has given us to better love and serve others in our various areas of responsibility in life. A well-grounded identity in Christ and a clearly defined vision of the life God is calling you to live are a start, but they don't automatically make life easier. Challenges will still come your way. Luther called these the "cross of our vocations." The difference is you're more prepared to face and overcome them.

Looking inside ourselves for strengths and weaknesses is an uncomfortable process. But having helped so many people through to the other side of it, I can tell you it's worth the discomfort. So, in the following pages, we'll unpack the Called2B coaching framework—a journey that helps people discover and begin to live out their God-given calling and purpose.

3

What Is Called2B?

How do you begin to unlock your divine potential to impact the world around you? This question is multifaceted. You can't answer it in a "Yes/No" form or even a single sentence. It often means one thing today and something different three years from now. Though there are exceptions, there's a general rule about questions like "Who am I?" or "What am I meant to do?" Some people answer them over time through a lengthy process of trial and error. I'm fond of a marketing maxim: "Test until you receive a signal." You'll gain confidence through the internal confirmation and external reactions of others when you find the bullseye.

To this end, I developed the Called2B coaching framework as I worked my way out of my own wilderness experience. Even though I benefited from several coaching models, it seemed valuable to develop a comprehensive, all-encompassing vocational coaching awareness framework that keeps uncertainty at an absolute minimum—a life hack, if you will. It is vitally important to show how your faith connects to and aligns with the rest of your life as you discover and engage your God-given (Divine) GPS (Gifts, Passions, and Strengths).

The Called2B coaching framework is designed to empower everyday believers to discover and live out their authentic calling in Christ to be a greater blessing in our world today. Its goal is to help anyone seeking clarity to translate their faith in Christ into action in daily life, in love and service to their neighbors. Called2B emphasizes the importance that faith must always precede our good works, or in other words, that our being must always precede our doing. I found that only after increasing a believer's awareness of their calling in Christ can they properly be empowered to live from their authentic self. How can a person suffering from amnesia know what to do in life if they don't know who they are? How can you?

In other words, is it possible to run ahead of God, thinking you know what he's called you to do, and end up doing more harm than good? In my experience—it can be. How else do you describe my story of accepting that pastoral call as I fled a bad situation only to find myself in another similarly bad circumstance? How could I possibly have been wrong to accept a position as a pastor in service to God's people?

Even so, this vocational coaching process goes beyond performance, tips and techniques, metrics, and ticking the boxes. If you truly want to partner with God in the unique calling he has for you, then you must be prepared to be transformed from the inside out.

This coaching framework did not come to me fully formed. It involved a great deal of time and trials to develop. Called2B is a product of pain—intense spiritual pain brought on by a lack of clarity in regards to my own identity and trying to navigate challenging circumstances, often on my own.

It took the sorrow of my own trials to help me better understand those suffered by others. My failures stirred up a reservoir of deep empathy and compassion for others on similar journeys. I now carry a long list of painful, unpleasant experiences to recall when I see someone wrestling with their calling. Martin Luther once stated, "Prayer, study, and suffering make a pastor." They also make a good coach.

Let's face it. No one would choose to go through the dark night of the soul if it could be avoided. That's why today, I've been called to this place to walk with others to navigate the uncertainty of discovering their calling in life in a far more meaningful and intentional way.

The vision of Called2B comprises three core elements: *identity, empowerment,* and *impact.*

Identity centers around being aware of who you are at your core. Too often, we struggle trying to do everything thrown our way. When you understand your God-given identity and workmanship, you will be more ready to face the world and its challenges because you know who you are and where your strengths lie. The following questions are worth pondering:

- How is it that identity so easily slips through our fingers, even if we think we have a sense of it?

- Why are some people able to remember their identity, even under pressure, while others seem to forget theirs as soon as they encounter resistance?

- How can believers stay grounded in identity as "who we are" (being) instead of "what we can accomplish" (doing)?

- What are the consequences of defaulting to our lifework, or professional excellence, as our identity? How do we damage our vertical and horizontal relationships when this happens?

You'll recall how I got my identity mixed up with the title of being a pastor. I thought I knew who I was until the ground shifted underneath me. I was trapped in an uncomfortable situation where my calling no longer felt like one. So what can a person do if their external source of identity suddenly fails them?

Of course, serving God's church had not suddenly or indeed become a burden. But I had given it the ability to influence, even govern, my sense of purpose and identity when it came to the core of my being. Unfortunately, I'd pinned too much of my identity to my paid professional role.

Radio host Dave Ramsey likes to say, "Either you happen to your money, or your money happens to you." It's a similar idea when it comes to identity. We will form one, for better or worse.

It might be a true identity or a false one. But it's not something we can sidestep or ignore without consequences. Called2B gives you the tools to build a seaworthy ship regarding your ultimate sense of identity—something you can cling to, even when the waves get rough. For the waves of life will get rough. It's just a matter of time.

Empowerment is the next element of Called2B. In this part of the coaching framework, you better understand your authentic identity, and the next question is how to practice better self-care. With empowerment, the goal is to help you develop a plan focused on caring for yourself and improving your overall wellness regarding your heart, soul, mind, and body.

We need to *be* before we *do*. To be effective in our daily areas of responsibility, we need to care for ourselves holistically. Rest is an essential part of caring for ourselves. Jesus declared in Mark 2:27 (NIV), "The Sabbath was made for man, not man for the Sabbath." Sabbath rest is a gift by God to humanity so that we can rest and remember whose we are in life. Reflect on your previous week and think about the upcoming week in a state of stillness and review. Did you slow down to rest? In an episode of the Called2B podcast, we asked: "Do we work from our rest, or do we rest from our work?"[1] People often keep going until they collapse and are forced to rest. However, being intentional about rest will allow you to show up at your best in your various callings to impact those around you more significantly.

The last element of the Called2B coaching framework is *impact*. Many wish to see improvement in the world, but they are unwilling to be that difference. Having an understanding of who we are and how we as individuals can live more authentically isn't enough. Now, we need to understand how we can impact those around us in what Luther called the four stations, or domains, of life: Family, Church, Lifework, and Society. Or, more simply, where we live, worship, work, and play. We can impact those people in these areas of life on a deeper level, whether it be a manager

---

1. Travis Guse, Trish Freshwater, and Kevin Scott, "Empowering Your Soul (Episode 15)," Feb 18, 2023, in *Called2B Podcast*, YouTube video, produced by Kendall Guse, 22:35, https://www.youtube.com/watch?v=oymc9eJSEeQ.

giving guidance to an employee, a parent giving love and support to a child trying to navigate a challenging relationship, or a friend helping a friend through a difficult situation. How we interact with those in direct contact with us makes a lasting impact on the world.

Being present in the lives of others takes energy and time. Exhaustion and frustration put us in no place to serve, either in the home, church, school, or the workplace. However, by deepening our awareness of our authentic identity and focusing intentionally on things that empower our wellness, God can use us effectively to love and serve our neighbors. Most people think of wealth and status as the image of success in our society. Yet, true success comes from knowing who you are and traversing the path you're meant to walk. This knowledge, in turn, gives us the power and energy to be a greater blessing to others in the world around us.

To help you discover and live out your unique calling in your various areas of responsibility in life, let me introduce you to the Called2B dashboard (see the image below). Much like your car's dashboard, this tool contains all the vital signs and critical measurements to know if your personal "engine" is running correctly and smoothly. So, for example, you would check your speed, oil, pressure, fuel level, engine temperature, and RPMs on the road. As you go through this discovery process, we will explore in depth how to utilize this tool to empower you for your callings in life.

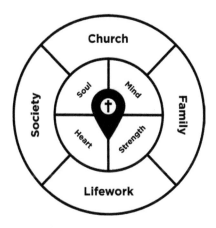

Called2B Coaching Dashboard

By using the Called2B dashboard, you can quickly assess the health and stability of your *authentic identity*, which comprises your *ultimate identity* in Christ (rather like a compass, understanding your true north) and your *unique identity* (Divine GPS to help you navigate your callings in life). You can also assess your *empowerment* regarding your self-care (how are you doing heart, soul, mind, and body?). Finally, you can evaluate your *impact* on those around you (those whom you have been called to bless in the four stations of life) by aiming your Divine GPS in love and service to others. The dashboard takes the mystery out of questions like "Who can I help?" and "Where should I serve?" Instead, the answers are far more straightforward.

You'll learn about each element of this coaching strategy in this book, which includes several tools to help you along the way. Using this framework, I've been able to help everyone, ranging from college students to business leaders to retirees, who needed encouragement and support in taking their next steps in life.

The following pages will walk you through each aspect of the Called2B coaching framework on a much deeper level and provide exercises for you to reflect upon to gain greater clarity about your calling.

4

Foundation of Called2B Framework
Relationships

WHILE CALLED2B IS A coaching framework designed to help everyday believers discover and live out their authentic calling in Christ, it would be important to lay the foundation of this coaching awareness model. This foundation lies in the fact that the entirety of our lives revolves around relationships. In fact, the longer I live, the more I truly believe that life is ultimately all about relationships. Think of how much your parents impacted you, for better or worse. Or how your spouse and children do, if you have them. You could find many books on the subject of relationships in a quick Google search. Your friends, family, teachers, boss, co-workers, neighbors, peers—even your children's friends—all of these people impact your life somehow. Each relationship takes differing amounts of energy and focus. And they influence different parts of your personality, helping to shape you into the person you are today.

God created human life to consist of a network of interdependent relationships where people give and receive care from one another. It happens when you sit, listen, and help a good friend overcome a challenge. You express pride in them and affirm their resilience. You give, and they receive. Even strangers have a relational influence on us in small but noticeable ways. Think of checking out in a grocery line. How you treat the cashier (and how they treat you) carries implications far beyond that encounter, whether for good or otherwise.

Have you ever watched people in a mall, at a park, or perhaps in a coffee shop? I love to do so while enjoying a latte. People-watching is a fun and interesting pastime. Give it a try sometime. You can tell a lot about one person's relationship with another by quietly observing them. If you do, think carefully about what you see. A wise observer always tries to understand how relationships affect individual responses. There's no such thing as someone acting alone, independent of all others, as an island all unto themselves.

A friend recently told me that he observed a pair of teenagers, male and female, in a waiting room. Within seconds, he could see by the girl's body language that it wasn't going well for her male companion, a potential suitor. He was trying to charm and interest her, and she was doing her best to ignore and rebuff his advances. I've seen a moment or two like this in my lifetime; they're awkward and cringeworthy. But they also speak volumes, frequently with little dialogue and no mic'd up tracks to hear what people are saying. The desire to connect with another person runs deep within us, yet our advances are only sometimes reciprocated. As embarrassed as you might feel for the young lady in the story, I also empathize with the young man as someone who has lived life a little longer. He made a public spectacle of himself, hoping to make a love connection, and (I imagine) went home feeling slightly less confident than he did at first.

Whether or not we like to admit it, we act (or react) based on our relationships with others and how they speak and behave toward us. That's easier to recognize when you're an outside observer rather than an active participant. But if you pay attention to the people around you, over time, you'll develop a literacy of the actions of others and (to some degree) their motives. You realize how frequently we think and behave in response to relational nuances. I recall how my transition from the calling of singleness to marriage exerted unseen and unspoken pressure to do things differently than I had in the past. It was no longer "just me," which meant there was an adjustment I had to make to correspond to the new reality of "we." To quote Jack Nicholson from the movie *As Good as It Gets*, my wife made me want to be a better man.

This principle holds even more true if you are a follower of Christ. In the tradition of Martin Luther, we understand our relational reality of life as our vertical and horizontal callings—or we can think of them in terms of relationships. I first learned to see my relationships in life through this bi-focal lens in seminary from Dr. Robert Kolb, one of my favorite professors. At the beginning of each class, he would set up the premise of a theological topic for us to examine and then open it for discussion. With him, we did more than study theology; we applied it to real-life situations. It was like lab work for theologians. We researched and thought deeply about each aspect of what we believe, teach, and confess and followed it up with exercises to get us to reflect, think, and act in real-life situations with the mind of Christ.

I enjoyed Dr. Kolb's questions. They compelled us to dig deeper into ourselves and the teachings of the church in ways different than we had before. His brightly colored socks would flash out at us as he swung his legs while sitting on his desk. He'd get a mischievous twinkle in his eye when he was about to say something profound. He dug into our reasoning and helped us question our gut reactions. His goal was to help us see things from a higher kingdom perspective. As a result, I learned more in his classes than in several years of ministry before. But the theological construct that stuck with me the most was that of our vertical and horizontal callings in life as believers.

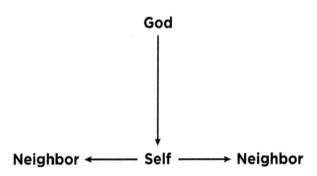

Vertical and Horizontal Callings

First, we have a *vertical calling* in heaven (a.k.a. "passive" righteousness): Our primary relationship with God is by grace through faith in Christ, which defines our ultimate sense of identity and empowers us to live out this ultimate calling in life. It was reading Rom 1:17 (NIV) that transformed Luther's understanding of what made him right in his relationship with God, "For in the gospel the righteousness of God is revealed—a righteousness that is by faith from first to last, just as it is written: 'The righteous will live by faith.'"

Second, we also have a *horizontal calling* on earth (a.k.a. "active" righteousness): Our secondary relationship with our neighbors and the social and relational responsibilities that go with it. For Luther, our callings as they relate to the horizontal relationships in this life are defined by these words of Paul in Gal 5:14 (NIV), "For the entire law is fulfilled in keeping this one command: 'Love your neighbor as yourself.'"

When Dr. Kolb taught us this theological concept, that of Luther's Two Kinds of Righteousness, a few things came into focus for me. I was struck by how much clarity there was when I viewed life in relational terms. When you see life through this lens, you realize just how deeply it permeates every decision and action you take.

We're often told that there isn't much that can make a person happy unless they have other people to share it with in life. Think of the sound of a good friend's laugh or the warm embrace of a child. What about that feeling you get when you know you can sit with someone and talk for hours? These things enrich our lives, and while having a human body makes someone material, they are far more profoundly spiritual. (By "spiritual," I refer simply to the soul, the invisible persona inside the human body that animates us.)

Let me give you an example of our vertical calling in heaven. This calling is your relationship with God through faith in Christ, both as it presently exists and as it is yet to become in eternity. Most religious traditions focus on what your relationship should look like with God. However, like the parental relationship with their child, that child does not have to work for their parents' love. The parents' love is simply a part of life and living. It is a solid foundation for the child to stand on and find security. God already loves us with an everlasting love in Christ, and that's all there is to it. And that love for you was demonstrated by Jesus on the cross at Calvary. God is your Father, and you, his beloved child! "See what great love the Father has lavished on us, that we should be called children of God! And that is what we are!" (1 John 3:1 NIV)

This love is not something we have to prove ourselves worthy of receiving. We receive it freely by grace through faith in Jesus (Eph 2:8–9). It is built-in, a foundation we can use for strength when we wonder if God genuinely loves us and is there for us, especially when we blow it and mess up in life.

But there's more to this puzzle called life. The second aspect of this relational nature of life is our horizontal calling on earth, represented by our connections to other people. This one can be difficult to navigate. Our day-to-day interactions with others can often feel disconnected from God, as though he doesn't notice or pay attention to them. These mainly occur in life's four areas of responsibility, according to Luther: Family, Church, Lifework, and Society. They could be a father or mother trying to earn money to put a meal on their family's table, volunteering in your local congregation, helping a coworker organize their filing system, or being a listening ear to your next-door neighbor in a difficult situation. This horizontal calling exists in and through our day-to-day lives. It's how we best use the gifts freely given to us by God to help those around us. And it's where we spend most of our time.

American culture tends to encourage people to look out for "number one" and to focus on themselves. As a result, we suffer from an epidemic of me-ism, which is at odds with the call of God to be sacrificial and practice generosity in our relationships with others. But love and service to one's neighbor are at the heart and soul of God's design and purpose for this life. So be advised—living out your calling in Christ in the horizontal reality of life is countercultural in today's world. It's an upstream swim.

It turns out we can only indeed look out for "number one" by looking out for everyone else in the first place. We truly are "our brother's (and sister's) keeper," after all (Gen 4:9). As we've already covered, no one is immune from the effect or influence of their relationships with others. If so, it follows that no one else is immune to the influence or impact you can exert on them, either. You have the ability to stir up reciprocity in them as easily as you can stir up animosity.

In other words, whether you choose to live selfishly or with generosity, the people in your orbit will feel the weight of it. They will have some reaction or response to your existence.

Their response to you can go one of a few ways. They might choose to ignore or ostracize you because you're silent and passive. They might become hostile or antagonistic in response to selfishness, rudeness, or aggression on your part. Or they might embrace and seek to include you because they know you as a blessing and a bringer of positive energy.

The point here is that you cannot have *zero* effect on anyone, not even those who appear ignorant or unaffected by you. Human existence doesn't work that way.

If it's true that you already have an effect on the people around you, the easiest way to improve it is to be more intentional when you interact with them. I challenge you to encourage one person daily for one week. Don't take the easy route here and say simple things like "Great job!" or "You look good today!" Get specific. Look at a coworker and say something detailed, like "The way you spoke to that client really showed how much of an expert you are, and I'm fortunate to learn from you." Or you can do this with your family, saying something like "That was brave of you to tell me how you feel. I know it isn't easy." We all walk around with empty buckets waiting to be filled. Find ways to add a drop of kindness to your daily interactions. The encounter will bless their day, and you will also be blessed in the process.

You'll be amazed at what happens when you sincerely encourage people. The deliberate emphasis on small details forces you to see people differently—and they do the same to you. It requires close observation and a longer-than-average span of attention. If you practice it for a week, you may notice how your words begin to affect their actions. For instance, your ability to see what others ignore can help someone face their unique challenges with confidence.

A wise sage once said, "I have learned much from my mentors. Even more from my peers. But I have learned the most from my students." When I look back on relationships in my life, several people have significantly impacted me in my life. However, I notice how the impact goes even deeper with the people I've coached. I see it most clearly in the lives of people who took and put into practice what we focused on during our coaching time together. They moved forward with the strengths they discovered, and I have the high privilege of bearing witness to the results.

Matt McEnerney stands out as one of those success stories. When I started writing my dissertation, I intended to use a case study approach—to focus on the stories of some of my previous coaching clients. I wanted to tell the story of three Millennials I worked with to explore the impact coaching could have on young people discovering and living out their calling in Christ in their daily lives. Matt was one of them, and he graciously agreed to let me share his story.

Matt was twenty-eight years old when I first met him. Uncertainty plagued him regarding what to do with his life. He had many interests, and we spent over nine months processing them together. He had ideas of what he wanted to do but needed help to settle on a single path. Over many months of coaching, Matt gained clarity about his gifts, passions, and strengths in life, as well as what it would look like to live them out in service to others.

He even began using the principles of coaching I modeled for him with the players of a baseball team he coached to help the players set personal and team goals. Unfortunately, the team had the worst offense in their league at the start of the season. However, they worked steadily through the season under Matt's coaching and ended up winning the league championship. Through our time together, Matt realized he had a gift to help people transcend their limitations. Seeing him awaken to this and then deploy it successfully was an eye-opening and life-giving experience for us both.

During our coaching together, Matt also began exploring his faith. Like many of his generation, he was a Christian nomad, not committed to any particular home church. Matt believed in God but wanted to understand what it practically meant in his daily life. As a result of coaching, he started to spend time daily studying God's word. Over time, our coaching relationship transformed into one of discipleship and close friendship. As he did when coaching his baseball team, Matt leveraged the strengths we uncovered in our sessions to establish himself in a church community where he could serve and thrive in his day-to-day life. By serving and offering himself from a place of strength, he built quality friendships and relationships in a thriving environment. Through his horizontal relationships, Matt was making a kingdom impact.

Tragically, Matt died in a car accident on the Fourth of July in 2019. When I heard the news, I was in disbelief and heartbroken. I lost a dear friend and brother in Christ that day. I'm grateful for the time we shared and everything he accomplished. And most of all, I find comfort in the fact that Matt died knowing the promises of the One who is the resurrection and the life (John 11:25).

In a Christmas card he sent me a few years before his passing, Matt reflected on our time coaching together:

"The gift of your time each week has been one of the best gifts and blessings I've ever received. It means more to me than you'll ever know. Your guidance and the light you've shed on my life have really opened up my eyes to what's truly important in life. I know we've spent a lot of time talking about me and my life, but your generosity and the way you live your life have been an inspiration to me and helped me to see what it really means to live a Christ-serving life."

I treasure that card to this day. When I first started coaching Matt many years ago, I was in the early stages of developing my Called2B coaching process. In fact, much of its development can be traced to what I learned in coaching individuals like Matt.

It was a web of relationships that led me to connect with Matt, who took what he'd learned from our coaching together into his sphere of influence in his love and service to others. I offered him what I'd learned from my interconnected set of resources and relationships. Then Matt used his strengths and gained knowledge to help an entire baseball team, his family, a church community, and so many others. The impact multiplied; our work now spreads to impact people I've never met through their connection to Matt.

Spiritual enrichment and blessings flow and trickle between us in the same way oxygen and nutrients travel throughout our bodies via the circulatory system. It's an interdependent system. The tug of a string here or a reinforcement there shapes how we grow and move about the world today. The human race is an immensely complex (and complicated) species. We rarely step outside of ourselves enough to see that each person around us is living a life completely different and separate from our own. But if you pause to consider the intricate ways people connect, the potency of relationships in our lives is breathtaking.

The idea of being connected through relationships doesn't mean we despise or ignore ourselves. In fact, I cannot stress enough the importance of self-care. Ultimately, self-care is not selfish because it empowers you to show up at your best for the sake of others in your various callings in life. Burnout is common among those who serve within helping professions for precisely this reason: they tend to ignore the importance of creating space to take time to rest and recharge. You cannot pour from an empty cup. If you spend all your time and resources giving to others, you'll soon find yourself empty on the inside. To truly serve our fellow human beings, we must be "full" ourselves.

Think of your vertical calling in heaven as a substance that fills your cup. Its baseline is God's love for us. When you submerge yourself in the reality of Jesus' love freely given to you by the working of the Holy Spirit and intentionally remember it in your daily life, you can live every day from a full and overflowing cup. If you're secure in God's abundant life for you in Christ, you can live out your horizontal callings to help others, filling their cups while God fills yours.

This reality leads to an essential question for you to consider: Who is filling your cup? We must remember the importance of surrounding ourselves with the right people to pour into our lives as we seek to pour into others. If you struggle to recognize or separate yourself from toxic or destructive influences, I recommend speaking to a pastor or a licensed therapy professional. There are specific challenges in life that coaching cannot help you to overcome. Removing these influences from your life because they stifle your growth can sometimes be one of them. Often, we are called by Jesus to love what I term EGRs (extra grace required), but we don't have to devote all our time and energy to them. At times, they can become like a black hole, sucking the life out of everything and everyone around them. On a journey of growth, the first people to take offense to your new behavior are the ones used to controlling, manipulating, or mistreating you. Don't let them stop you. Instead, surround yourself with those who are like shining stars who give life to others by reflecting the light of Christ's love.

Make a list of the most significant relationships in your life. Look specifically at the four areas of responsibility: Family, Church, Lifework, and Society. Now, divide them into two columns: people who fill your cup and those who drain it. While you can still be kind and courteous toward those listed in column two, you don't need to explain or apologize. But it's time to treat drainers differently. I like to say, "Don't water the brown grass; water the green grass instead." It doesn't sound politically correct to modern ears; however, Jesus encourages us not to cast our pearls before swine

(Matt 7:6). Basically, he is saying not to offer others what they cannot appreciate.

Now, let's move on to column one—the people who appreciate and are receptive to what you have to offer. These are people who uplift you, encourage and challenge you in constructive ways. When Jesus sent out his disciples two by two, he instructed them to look for people of peace (Matt 10:11; Luke 10:6). These are people who are not only receptive to what you have to offer but, in turn, they show care and concern for you as well. In column one are people I can talk to for hours one day and not hear from them for a few months, but when we're together again, we pick right back up on a shared journey of growth. So, who are the people in your world that come to mind? Circle anyone in column one you'd like to be around more often.

On the flip side, observe column two. Take a moment to think about the names you entered. Why did you choose them? How do they make you feel? What do they say or do that drains you of your time and energy? These questions will help you determine whether it's worth an honest conversation or if these issues are a part of who this person is at their core. If you cannot suitably address it, the question follows: Is there a way you can spend less time with them? It's not that you don't care or shouldn't love and serve them, because Jesus loves them, too. Instead, it is learning to invest your time and energy wisely in those who value and appreciate what you have to offer and vice versa.

Taking the time to build healthy, reciprocating, growth-oriented relationships is essential for your wellness. The people around you should celebrate your wins and support you through your losses. This concept is known as a "virtuous circle." The people inside column one grow together and get positive energy from spending time together. They sometimes take a lot of work to find and cultivate, but you must understand that who you spend time with is entirely under your control, even if it doesn't feel like it. Reclaiming that power and choosing your web of relationships will impact your future, for better or worse.

5

Connecting the Relationship Dots

For one of my earliest coaching clients, Dave Drever, understanding where to focus living out his calling in Jesus in regards to his relationships, after being coached through the beginning foundations of the Called2B framework, helped him tremendously in navigating an uncertain territory: Hollywood.

At only twenty-three years of age, Dave moved from Sacramento to Southern California to work for a production company, where he quickly found himself close to the fine line of compromising his integrity, often on a daily basis. He was part of the team that produced several music videos for the hip-hop artist Snoop Dogg, and along with it came offers of work in the adult film industry. Dave felt uncomfortable. He had grown up as an active member of the church his family attended in Sacramento. This environment was at odds with how he wanted to live out his life and faith.

When Dave approached me for help and discernment, I suggested we work together in a coaching relationship for a season. The way forward wasn't clear initially, but I felt confident that if we worked diligently, God would help us make discoveries and find solutions aligned with Dave's authentic identity in Christ. I knew him well enough to know that the solution and expertise actually lay inside him rather than in me. As long as we remained open to the guidance of the Holy Spirit, we could rely on the grace of God every step of the way.

Some time into our coaching sessions together, Dave grew in his understanding of the prevailing culture in Hollywood, which is best characterized by the question, "What can you do for me?" Behind the exterior, that's what many people in the entertainment industry want to know.

Dave observed that while most people silently ask that question, not many people know the answer! Suddenly, this clarified a significant opportunity for a servant-hearted leader like Dave. All he had to do was prime the pump by working with (and from) a slightly different question: "What can I do for you?" As his acquaintances and friends in Hollywood encountered this willing and generous spirit, they were stunned. Who comes to Hollywood with that kind of attitude? Who would survive?

Five years later, Dave got an opportunity to partner with a major Hollywood talent agency to start a new faith-based media company called Freely. You know you're onto something when big Hollywood companies invest in a faith-driven enterprise! Five years after signing the deal Freely's first media project, *The Long Goodbye: The Kara Tippitts Story*, launched on Netflix.

Furthermore, by serving and loving people in Hollywood, Dave learned how to disarm the standard defenses against the Christian faith. He borrowed on that timeless principle of reciprocity—as Jesus once told the apostles, "Freely you have received; freely give" (Matt 10:8 NIV). With each act of selflessness and benevolence, Dave won opportunities to share Christ with people who would typically rebuff traditional evangelistic approaches. To this day, he hides in plain sight as a missionary in Hollywood. Called2B has helped Dave connect the dots of his vertical relationship with Jesus and how that translated into his horizontal relationships to love and serve his neighbors—those he comes into contact with on a daily basis.

6

Your Ultimate Identity

THE BEGINNING OF THE Called2B coaching framework is *identity*, because to move forward to a meaningful and purpose-filled life, you must first understand who you are outside of work, study, politics, or other labels that so commonly define us in our society. Identity describes who you are as a person, to the core of your being. It connects believers to their authentic identity, which consists of their *ultimate* and *unique identities*. Let me tell you a bit about each.

In Eph 2:8–9 (NIV), we hear, "For it is by grace you have been saved, through faith—and this is not from yourselves, it is the gift of God— not by works, so that no one can boast." Your ultimate identity is grounded in your calling from God that is by grace through faith in Jesus. There is nothing you have to do or can to do to establish this vertical relationship—it is all Jesus all the time!

Faith is what you truly believe, deep down in the core of your being, in the same way you believe that the cashier at the grocery store will accept your ten dollar bill in exchange for groceries. You never question or think about it because that's just the way it is. You'd be shocked if the cashier said, "I'm sorry, we don't accept money." Not only that, your faith in our currency would be undermined.

If we thought the same way about how God views us, "God loves and forgives me, and that's just the way it is," we genuinely exercise *faith*. At its core, "faith" means "trust." You trust in a God who proved himself trustworthy in the person and saving work of Jesus.

Another way we can measure our faith is to examine who and what influences our life, day-to-day. What positive voices do you listen to? A believer in God may cite Scriptures or church sermons. But every one of us, believer or not, listens to voices that contribute to (or diminish) who we are in our self-perception. The music we listen to, the things we read, and the people we talk with are examples of these voices. We have a choice in these things. We choose the enrichment we take the time to consume. They will shape how deeply we accept (or refuse) the truth of Scripture. As Pastor Jentezen Franklin says, "The right voices lead to the right choices."[1] The right voices, more importantly, lead you to the right identity.

Your choice of influences says a lot about who you are as a person. It doesn't have to be inspirational, business-centric, or even holy words that fill you up. But be warned—*someone* will grab the "loudspeaker" into your life if you don't make an intentional choice about who you listen to on a daily basis.

Then, there are the messages you send to yourself. In our crazed, modern culture, they usually sound like self-reproach ("I *should* be so much more than I am!") or panic at the prospect of falling behind ("I *can't* take a day off!"). Even if we don't mutter them under our breath, we send these messages silently—by being relentlessly busy, distracted by technology, and leaving no margin in our lives.

What messages do you send yourself, either verbally or through your habitual actions? What have you done to feed your interests and passions or bring rest and recuperation to your soul today? It could be waking up to watch the sunrise or reading a devotion with a good cup of coffee. Or painting, even if you do it poorly. You could go for a walk or lie under a tree to watch light filter through the leaves.

1. Jentezen Franklin, "Right Voice, Right Choice," sermon, November 16, 2019, https://www.youtube.com/watch?v=SodJSE-k8MI.

In those moments, what words do you speak to yourself? It's important to ask how you *interpret* life around you. What do you think or say when you make a mistake or when things don't go your way? What happens when someone brighter, more skilled, more attractive, or more influential comes into your orbit? Do you admire or envy them? Either way, you're sending messages to yourself. The only thing that matters is what *kind* of messages you send.

Along with recognizing significant positive voices, it is essential also to understand the negative voices we allow into our lives. These voices might undermine how we truly want to live our lives. Is there someone in your ear telling you that you aren't good enough or urging you to point fingers and blame others for your pain? Are you surrounded by hate and anger, either from the media you consume or within your own family? And, of course, negative voices can also be silent ones. Negativity can be found in ignoring our own needs and wants.

Conversely, negative voices can also come in the form of questions. Take, for example, the voice of the crafty serpent in the book of Genesis, who questioned Eve: "Did God really say, 'You must not eat from any tree in the garden'?" By questioning the goodness of God and his promises, Adam and Eve traded their God-given identity as the beloved children of the Father for a lie. This is the very first instance of identity theft!

Many things in life offer a sense of identity with the promise of life and meaning. People seek identity through possessions, reputation, recognition, or the positions and titles they hold. However, these things do not build up our identity. Ask any athlete who was last year's champion, any billionaire on their deathbed, any washed-up celebrity, or a former national leader. These things come and go, yet a God-given identity is *permanent*. In explaining the first of the Ten Commandments (Exod 20:3), Martin Luther said in his explanation of the First Commandment, about having no other gods but God alone, that whatever we look to as first in our life for our highest good—for our ultimate sense of identity, security, and meaning in life—is, in fact, our god. So, whose voice are you listening to in terms of your identity? Is it God's or someone else's?

If you are struggling with your ultimate sense of your identity, wondering who you are and where your worth is found, then hear the voice of God to you this day. Your identity is established through faith alone in Jesus and his saving work. The apostle Paul says in Gal 3:26–27 (NIV), "So in Christ Jesus you are all children of God through faith, for all of you who were baptized into Christ have clothed yourselves with Christ." Your ultimate identity is now located in Jesus, through whom you are restored to your original created identity as a "son or daughter" of God. You are his child by grace through faith and nothing in all the world can separate you from that ultimate identity found in Jesus. It is so easy to forget this baptismal identity, so make sure to intentionally remember it daily.

Not only have you been freely given this individual identity as a child of God, but you now have a collective identity together with all believers. Through your vertical relationship to God in Christ, you are also given a new identity as being part of the "royal priesthood." We read in 1 Pet 2:9 (ESV), "But you are a chosen race, a royal priesthood, a holy nation, a people for his own possession, that you may proclaim the excellencies of him who called you out of darkness into his marvelous light." You are chosen! You are a son or daughter of the King! You are holy! You are his possession! Now, go out secure in that identity as part of the Priesthood of All Believers as you reflect the light of his goodness and love through all of your callings in life.

To better understand how you see yourself in terms of your ultimate identity, ask the following questions:

1. When you were younger, who did you most want to be like and why?

2. Not including your faith, what things, both positive and negative, are informing your identity in your life? What voices are you listening to?

3. How does your identity from these voices inform how you see yourself and navigate life?

4. How would you like to see yourself? How would you like to be different when it comes to your identity?

Head over to called2b.com/identity to download your free supplemental questionnaire to reflect more on your ultimate identity.

The second part of your *authentic identity* is discovering and understanding your *unique identity*. This step in the Called2B coaching framework connects you to your *horizontal* callings in life, which we defined earlier as the secondary horizontal relationships within the realm of earth and the social and relational responsibilities that go with it. *Unique identity* is all about identifying key aspects of ourselves that make up who we are according to God's workmanship and design—including the Gifts of our personality, Passions, and Strengths. This gifting and design is what I term as your *Divine GPS*, which we will unpack in the next section of this book.

7

Your Unique Identity

Divine GPS

BEFORE THE INVENTION OF GPS technology, driving somewhere new took a lot of work. You either had a (hopefully up-to-date) map, or you asked directions and tried to remember them while you drove (unless you wrote them down). Or, in the case of my wife and I, one of us could read maps while the other lacked that spatial gifting. We learned very early on in our relationship that she should be the driver and I should be the map reader whenever we are going to unfamiliar places. This compromise and recognition of gifting between us avoided many fights.

Map reading was indeed inefficient at best, especially when driving alone. Many found themselves lost in new surroundings. We would have to ask complete strangers for directions or drive around in circles if our pride prevented us from asking for help. And even if you had a map, trying to read it while driving was dangerous and difficult. We often tried to stop, look at the map, get to the next landmark, stop again, look at the map, and so forth.

Then came GPS. As the roads "appeared" online, we could now quickly plug in an address and select "take me there" to get step-by-step directions to our destination. As GPS improved, we could get alerts for slow traffic, construction, and even speed traps. Today, GPS is a part of everyday life. I have no doubt that I would safely be able to get into my car, plug in a location across the country, and make it there with ease. I feel comfortable during the journey instead of the pressure of trying to reach the correct destination.

Believe it or not, God thought to include a similar system within you as part of his workmanship and design in your life. His *Divine GPS* in you has a similar goal: you can get the same sense of security to navigate through life when you know how you have been gifted and what truly matters to you. Armed with these tools, you can be in entirely new situations—talking to new people, heading in new directions, and, yet, you will feel steady within yourself. Life is simpler when you know what you can or cannot handle.

Opportunities arise that play to your gifts, and you know to raise your hand in seconds. A situation materializes that runs against your values, and you withdraw without giving it another thought. You understand how you influence others around you, so you have a better sense of when to offer your strength. If things take a turn for the worse, you don't freak out and blame yourself, nor do you play the blame game. You provide leadership, or you become a helpful and steady supporter of whoever does.

A coaching client of mine, Manoj, wanted to start a business but wasn't sure what he should offer. He had previously worked and consulted for a few tech companies and had some time between gigs to think about what he wanted to do next. Together, we worked to discover his Gifts, Passions, and Strengths. I noticed Manoj's entrepreneurial spirit. He understood business and the concepts it took to create a thriving company. He knew a lot about the market and had read hundreds of books on entrepreneurship and business development. But even with all this knowledge of *how* to make a business successful, he still couldn't figure out *what* this new business would offer.

Manoj knew he needed to build a business aligned with his unique identity. When we worked through the CliftonStrengths® Assessment, we found his top two strengths were "Ideation®" and

"Strategic®."[1] Now, CliftonStrengths® defines Ideation® as people who are fascinated by ideas. They are able to find connections between seemingly disparate phenomena. So, we knew his company would involve people turning their ideas into reality. Then we looked at his Strategic® talent. CliftonStrengths® describes Strategic® as the ability to see patterns and identify alternatives, even if others only see a perplexing situation. Combining these strengths with Manoj's passion for entrepreneurship, he concluded that his company could be an entrepreneurial training company. It could help business owners design and execute winning strategies for growth.

Once Manoj understood his Gifts, Passions, and Strengths, I coached him through creating a plan for him to move forward. That plan and the understanding of his internal GPS have allowed Manoj to build a successful multifaceted company called Think-Tomi that helps train people in Silicon Valley to start and grow their entrepreneurial ventures.

Each part of who we are plays a function in forming our Divine GPS, an internal roadmap, as we seek to live out our calling in Christ in our various callings in life. This Divine GPS consists of the Gifts of our personality, Passions, and Strengths, which then combine to form our unique identity.

To further illustrate this concept of our Divine GPS, I offer the following analogy.

Your *Gifts* are like the "personality" of the driver. It is how you drive a car. Do you have a lead foot—are you a "doer" who keeps their foot on the gas pedal? Do you slip quickly in and out of traffic with confidence, or are you hesitant to merge? Do you slow down and give people space to merge, or do you speed up and assert your right of way? Just imagine, you might assume one type of driver personality when encountering a Ferrari and another when you see an electric car. Every car is designed with a purpose in mind, and each driver's personality correlates to the type of car they choose to drive. It is the same for the Gifts that God gives and shapes within human beings in terms of their personality.

1. Gallup®, CliftonStrengths® and the CliftonStrengths 34 Themes of Talent are trademarks of Gallup, Inc. All rights reserved.

Your *Passions* are like gas in the car. They're the fuel to get you going. It's your *why*. As with auto fuel, you can have different levels of octane or different levels of passion. One passion outranks another. You may enjoy golf at an economy level, like 87-octane gasoline. You play it once or twice a month with friends, and you enjoy it. Yet, if you had to play it every day, you'd burn out.

The enthusiasm factor may kick up a notch, however, if you have a passion for public speaking. Now, you have an audience and an opportunity to impart wisdom and understanding. People see you as an authority, and they're eager to absorb knowledge through your stories and information. You've now struck high-performance passion like rocket fuel.

Finally, your *Strengths* are those God-given talents representing the abundance of performance you can render in certain situations. Consider your talents as what you do best to the design and performance of a car. For example, a Corvette can run rings around a 4x4 on a smooth, flat surface. Yet, take the two vehicles off-road, and you can imagine which one you'd rather have. This understanding helps us know what roads in our callings in life we are designed to handle and what roads we aren't.

Let's now go over how to discover your Divine GPS. In the following sections, I will provide links for you to take each assessment I recommend. Once you've taken the assessments and received your results, consider going through the questionnaire tools on my website, Called2B.com, to help you think through how to use the information. By going through these exercises with an open heart and honest answers, you will get the best results that genuinely speak to your authentic self.

GIFTS

Let's begin by looking at the Gifts of our personality. I use the phrase "Gifts" plural because, essentially, our personality is made up of two parts: the first being our *temperament*, which God hardwires in us, and the second being our *character*, which can be shaped. You could compare them to a computer's hardware (wires,

CPU, motherboard) and software (the programs and apps stored in its memory).

To the long-standing question of whether personality results from nature or nurture, the simple answer to this question is "Yes." One portion of personality is innate, which is part of God's design and workmanship, known as our temperament. The other is shaped through our stories, relationships, and interaction with the world, and it's called our character.

Thus, personality is both innate and shaped. This gift of God's workmanship and working is not just one's physical form but each aspect of who we are as a person at the core of our being. The exploration of one's personality is vital, as it has an impact not only on what one does in their various callings in life but also on how we go about our relationships with others.

Your personality directly relates to how you interact with the world around you. Having a solid understanding of your personality helps you understand where you fit best and how you can be the greatest blessing to others.

I use two assessments to help clients understand the Gifts of their personality within their Divine GPS—the DISC assessment (effective for measuring a person's temperament) and the VIA (Values In Action) Character Strengths Survey (for evaluating a person's character strengths and values in life). Both of these assessments help create self-awareness when their questions are answered honestly. Many times, when a client goes through them, they're amazed at how well these assessments describe them at the end.

Remember, the goal of these assessment tools is to create awareness around God's gifting in your life and to put certain traits of your personality into words where you have trouble doing it. These assessments are well-written and developed by professionals in the field of psychology, specifically designed to help people understand more about themselves and how they tick.

Let's start with the DISC assessment. Based on the work of Carl Jung, DISC is a well-known and widely used tool for better understanding your temperament. DISC assessment measures two different dichotomies of your personality.

The first dichotomy helps you understand if you have a preference for being an Extrovert (energized by being with others, drained by being alone, outwardly stimulated, quicker to decide and act, talking thoughts out loud) or being an Introvert (energized by being alone, drained by being around others, inwardly stimulated, think first before speaking). The other dichotomy the DISC assessment measures for is if you are Relationship-Oriented (valuing the feelings and thoughts of others, more flexible in personal beliefs, more prone to procrastinate on tasks in order to socialize, tend to be more values and people-centered in decision making, emotionally warm to many) or if you are Task-Oriented (value work and getting things done, strong sense of personal convictions, putting work ahead of spending time with others, more logical in decision making, emotionally warm to a few).

Within the intersection of these two dichotomies, the DISC assessment deepens your awareness about which of the four temperament styles is your style when it comes to your personality. Often, these overflow with one another so that someone may be high in one temperament style and then have one or two minor temperament styles from an adjacent category. The four temperament styles are as follows:

1. Dominant (D) is characterized as those who are Extroverted and Task-Oriented.

2. Influence (I) is characterized as those who are Extroverted and People-Oriented.

3. Steady (S) is characterized as those who are Introverted and People-Oriented.

4. Compliant (C) is characterized as those who are Introverted and Task-Oriented.

Here is a brief overview of the two dichotomies and four temperaments of the DISC assessment:

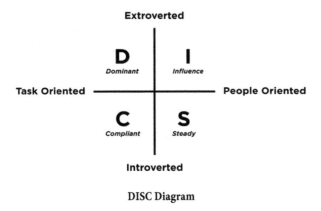

DISC Diagram

By studying these personality dichotomies and tempera-ment styles, you can understand your personality better and your impact on others. Whether working on a team, searching for the right career, interacting with family, or developing social skills, I've found them very helpful in finding your best fit and the impact you can make in your various areas of responsibility in life.

For example, when considering a career, if you are a high D, you might find a good fit serving as a lawyer, police officer, or the CEO of a corporation. If you are a high I, you might consider a career as a writer, graphic artist, or marketing professional. While there are also other factors to consider regarding your Divine GPS, understanding your temperament can get you pointed in the right direction when considering what you would do for a living.

The following are some potential coaching questions to ex-plore around the DISC assessment:

1. What things do you do well? What things don't you do well?

2. How do you re-energize yourself after a long day?

3. How do you approach your relationships with others?

4. Which do you enjoy more, working on tasks or working with people?

While there are a number of DISC assessments in the mar-ketplace, I have found the Christian DISC especially helpful in working with everyday believers due to its insights from Scripture and emotional intelligence. To take the Christian DISC assessment, go to called2b.com/christiandisc. Once the assessment is completed, head back to called2b.com/disc to download your free supplemental questionnaire.

The next assessment tool to help you better discern the Gifts of your personality is the VIA Character Strengths Survey.[2] This assessment tool helps participants deepen their awareness of their character strengths and values. Your character is ultimately a reflection of your values in action, those things that are important to you in life. Often, those I coach find that their lives don't align with those things they say are truly important to them. In this case, either life has gotten away from them, or their perceived values are not their actual values after all.

Growing out of the research of the new field of positive psychology, Christopher Peterson and Martin Seligman led a team of fifty-five researchers to answer the question, "What does good character mean, and how can it be measured?" During their research, they found six core virtues across different cultural and religious traditions, which include twenty-four character strengths within them. Biblically, there is a strong correlation between many of these character strengths and virtues and the fruit of the Spirit as described by the apostle Paul in Gal 5:22–23 along with the kingdom virtues of faith, hope, and love as described again by Paul in 1 Cor 13:13.

Ultimately, our character and virtues are shaped by our vision for life. As one lives a life aimed at some goal of living or becoming, one's virtue and character is shaped and formed for good or bad. So, what is the goal that we as believers should aim for in living a virtuous life? It is to live the life that we, as humanity, were originally created and are now redeemed to be in Christ, and at the end of time will define us for eternity in the new creation. In 2 Cor 5:17 (ESV) we hear, "Therefore, if anyone is in Christ, the new creation has come: The old has gone, the new is here!" As a new creation through faith in all that Jesus has done for our life and salvation,

2. www.viacharacter.org.

our goal as believers is to grow in this vision of Christ-likeness as we seek to love and serve our neighbors in our various areas of responsibility in life. In short, it is learning what it means to be fully human the way God always intended us to be and as Jesus was on our behalf.

Why is better understanding, developing, and harnessing your character strengths so important? The reason is that our character helps us chart our unique course in life, not only in how we live but also in our love and service to our neighbors. Knowing our character strengths also helps us engage better in our callings in life and allows us to show up as the best version of ourselves. Our character is especially important when facing adversity and challenges in life. It is a source of strength we can tap into to help us navigate difficult times. Ultimately, our character shows forth most clearly when people aren't looking. Finally, through the living out of our character we can bring glory to God. Character matters!

Here are VIA's classification of their twenty-four character strengths and six virtues:

Wisdom	Courage	Humanity	Justice	Temperance	Transcendence
Creativity	Bravery	Love	Teamwork	Forgiveness	Appreciation of Beauty & Excellence
Curiosity	Perseverance	Kindness	Fairness	Humility	Gratitude
Judgment	Honesty	Social Intelligence	Leadership	Prudence	Hope
Love of Learning	Zest			Self-Regulation	Humor
Perspective					Spirituality

To take the free VIA Character Strengths Survey go to https://www.viacharacter.org/. Once you have your results, head over to called2b.com/via to download the supplemental questionnaire, so you can unpack your discovery.

Below are some starting questions to help you think about your VIA results:

1. How accurately do your VIA results reflect the essence of who you are at your core in terms of your character?

2. Which VIA character strengths have people recognized in you in the past?

3. What do you sense are those things that you value as a result of your VIA character strengths? What kind of things are important to you in life?

4. How do you see yourself living out your VIA character strengths in your life currently (personally, family, career, church, community, etc.)?

PASSIONS

The second component of the Divine GPS is Passions. At its core, passion is *love* for something, either good or bad.

The great heroes of faith in the Bible displayed passion. You can see it with Moses, in his passion to see his people freed from the hand of Pharaoh. David had a passion for building a house for God. Solomon passionately pursued wisdom. And Paul was passionate about seeing all humanity saved by grace through faith, both Jews and Gentiles. In this part of the Called2B process, believers explore how their passions can be harnessed as they discover and live out their horizontal callings in life. Passion can fuel a person, especially when things get difficult. It can also unite people in common service to make a greater difference than they can individually.

To help believers better discern their passions in life, I invite you to take the Called2B Passion Assessment. Of all the assessment tools out there, I wanted one that got to the foundational interests, issues, and topics that genuinely speak to people at a soul level. I want to empower individuals to assess what is burning on their inside. A Passion can be something that excites you, or it can take the form of a deep burden you feel in your heart. It is Gabrielle Hamen-Kieffer in her book *Thriverorship*[3] who explains the power of tapping into your passions to fuel your callings in life when she says, "Your passions are the flame that warm and ignite your talents, values, and, most importantly, your purpose."

So, in this Passion Assessment, you'll encounter three separate grids. Each one covers different types of passions:

1. People Passions—What people do I have a heart for?

2. Issue Passions—What issues or concerns do I feel most strongly about?

3. Interest Passions—What interests excite me the most?

Circle anywhere from three to five of the topics that interest you the most in each grid in order to get a strong understanding of where your passions lie.

Once you have circled the topics that most interest you, you should tally nine to fifteen selections. Now we're getting somewhere; you're narrowing your field of focus based on people and subjects that *already* matter to you. From these nine to fifteen selections, try to identify your top three to five passions in your life. If you can find meaningful work that engages with a few of them, you'll quickly make a few solid steps in the right direction.

People Passion—What people do I have a heart for?
(Limit answers to 3 to 5)

Abuse Victims	Divorced	Men	Parents	Street Kids
Adults	Empty Nesters	Middle Schoolers	Parents of Teens	Teen Moms
Business Professionals	Engaged Couples	Minority Communities	Prisoners	Teens
Career Women	Grieving	The Poor	Seekers	Unemployed

3. Gabrielle Hamen-Kieffer, *Thriveorship* (Edina, MN: Beaver's Pond, 2005), 127.

Called2B

Children	Homeless	New Believers	Seniors	Visitors To Church
College Students	Hospitalized	New Church Members	Single Parents	Widows & Widowers
Couples	Infants	New Parents	Singles	Women
Disabled	Immigrants	Newlyweds	Gen Z	Millennials
Veterans	Refugees	Shut Ins	Orphans	Other

Issue Passion—What issue(s) or concern(s) do I feel most strongly about?
(Limit answers to 3 to 5)

Abortion Awareness	Discipleship	Marriage Issues	Housing	Racism
Addictions	Divorce Care	Ministry Involvement	Human Rights	Reaching the Lost
Administration	Economics	Overseas/ Domestic Missions	Hunger	Social Issues
AIDS	Education	Parenting	Injustice	Technology
The Arts	The Environment	Politics	International Issues	Teen Concerns
Child Care	Family Issues	Poverty	Interpersonal Relations	Terminal Illness
Counseling	Financial Issues	Disaster Relief	Legal Issues	Violence
Creative Projects	Health Care	Prisons	Literacy	Worship
Defending The Faith	Sexual Identity Issues/ LGBTQ+	Community Development	Immigration	Other

Interest Passion—What interest(s) excite you the most?
(Limit answers to 3 to 5)

Movies/Film Making	Music	Books	Science	Sports
Outdoors	Business	Fashion	Medical Field	Personal Health/ Fitness
Personal Development	Drawing/ Painting	Teaching	Faith/ Religion	Woodworking
Writing	Engineering	Hospitality	Sightseeing/ Travel	Cooking/ Baking
Wine/Beer	Entrepreneurship	Playing Games	Knitting/ Sewing	Hiking/ Camping
Biking	Walking/ Running	Dining Out	Collecting	Theater/ Acting
Shopping	Interior Design	Architecture	Mentoring/ Life Coaching	Psychology
Social Media	Graphic Design	Web Development	Sports Coaching	Public Service
Leadership/ Management	Organizational Development	Gardening/ Farming	Coffee/Tea	Other

The following are some questions to help explore your passions after you complete the Called2B Passion Assessment:

1. What things get you excited about waking up in the morning?

2. What topics could keep you up all night talking?

3. What things captured your imagination as a child? How do those things still capture your imagination?

4. What life experiences give you the most enjoyment, fulfillment, or satisfaction?

Take the Called2B Passion Assessment above and once you have your results, download the supplemental questionnaire at called2b.com/passion.

STRENGTHS

The third piece to better discerning your Divine GPS is to discover your God-given talents or Strengths. The CliftonStrengths® assessment (a.k.a. StrengthsFinder®) aids people in identifying their innate talents—their natural patterns of thoughts, feelings, and behaviors that can be productively applied in life.[4] This assessment measures for thirty-four distinct talent themes, or unique combinations of talents, that are universal to all people. Ultimately, the CliftonStrengths® Assessment helps you know what you do well in life and in what ways you can make the most significant impact in the lives of others. The way to take a talent and develop it as a strength in your life is known by Gallup® as the Strengths Equation:

The Strength Equation

Talent + Knowledge + Skills + Experience =

Strength

These talents are given to you as a gift of God's grace as part of his workmanship and design in your life. To serve one another with the strengths God provides is to play a role in God's economy. He uses each person to bless others uniquely according to their God-given ability. Each of us should utilize those Strengths that have been gifted to us to love and serve our Creator by loving and serving others. Just as the apostle Peter wrote in 1 Pet 4:10–11 (NIV), "Each of you should use whatever gift you have received to serve others, as faithful stewards of God's grace in its various forms . . . so that in all things God may be praised through Jesus Christ."

Below are the thirty-four talent themes of the Clifton-Strengths® Assessment, categorized into the four domains of

---

4. Gallup®, CliftonStrengths® and the CliftonStrengths 34 Themes of Talent are trademarks of Gallup, Inc. All rights reserved.

Strengths: Executing, Influencing, Relationship Building, and Strategic Thinking.[5]

Executing	Influencing	Relationship Building	Strategic Thinking
Achiever®	Activator®	Adaptability®	Analytical®
Arranger®	Command®	Developer®	Context®
Belief®	Communication®	Connectedness®	Futuristic®
Consistency®	Competition®	Empathy®	Ideation®
Deliberative®	Maximizer®	Harmony®	Input®
Discipline®	Self-Assurance®	Includer®	Intellection®
Focus®	Significance®	Individualization®	Learner®
Responsibility®	Woo®	Positivity®	Strategic®
Restorative™		Relator®	

To take the Top-5 CliftonStrengths® Assessment, go to https://store.gallup.com/p/en-us/10108/top-5-cliftonstrengths. Take the survey and download the results to help you understand your personal Strengths and how to use them. Gallup® also offers a podcast and a wealth of resources for learning how to use your top five strengths.[6] At called2b.com/cliftonstrengths, you'll find an accompanying questionnaire to help you take a deeper dive into your God-given talents and apply them to your callings in life.

The following are some questions to explore once you have completed the CliftonStrengths® Assessment:

1. As you review your CliftonStrengths® results, how well do they describe you and what you do best in life?

2. Of all the things you do well in life, what are one or two things that you do especially well? What correlation do you see with your CliftonStrengths® talents?

5. See Jim Collison in *The CliftonStrengths© Podcast*, produced by All Gallup© Webcast, https://podcasts.apple.com/us/podcast/the-cliftonstrengths-podcast/id1603713280.

6. Gallup®, CliftonStrengths® and the CliftonStrengths 34 Themes of Talent are trademarks of Gallup, Inc. All rights reserved.

3. Which parts of your current calling(s) in life do you enjoy the most and why?

4. From your top five results, what talents do you use in your current calling(s)? How do they help you live out these areas of responsibility?

Your Divine GPS is core to who you are and how you interact with the world around you. It's the foundation for the next steps within the Called2B process—*empowerment* and *impact*. In the following pages, I will give you the tools to create a life plan with the knowledge you gained from finding your Divine GPS.

Working through these assessments takes a lot of honest reflection about ourselves and our actions. You should celebrate that you took the time to work through them; not everyone does! I've worked with enough clients to know that you are most likely seeking to be transformed not only in your doing but also in your being. I understand that there may be a lot of emotion that comes with doing this kind of work. But by picking up this book and working through each step of the process, you've already proved you have the desire to transform your life. So take a break, grab your favorite beverage, and let's dive into *empowerment*.

8

Empowering Yourself

EMPOWERMENT IS THE CONNECTION point or the intersection between our relationship with God and our relationship with our neighbor. According to Jesus in Luke 10:27 (NIV), these are the two greatest commandments—to "Love the LORD your God with all your heart, and with all your soul, and with all your strength, and with all your mind, and, Love your neighbor as yourself." To become empowered for these two callings, you must build *awareness, commitment, practice,* and *accountability*. These are not easy to create or control, but they are the key differentials between people who dream about their calling versus people who actually *answer* it.

Each person has to take time to create their own customized empowerment plan. It is not only about working out and eating right (as crucial as these are to do). It has to do with building consistent actions and habits that revive, rejuvenate, and elevate your wellness and well-being. One person may need to sit in a hot tub for an hour. Others may need to paint or plant a garden. These things may not generate income, but that doesn't mean they're not worth doing. When we give all our time only to work or family, when will we find time to care for ourselves?

Let's take a look at developing an empowerment plan. When coaching my clients, I ask them to divide their plan into four unique phases: *building awareness, building commitment, building practice,* and *building accountability.* The exercises for each of them will be detailed later, but for now, I'll tell you a little bit about each one.

The first part of empowerment is *building awareness.* You start by learning about the 4 Aspects of Self (*heart, soul, mind, strength*) and how they affect your wellness. You rate yourself within each category to get a rough idea of how well you're currently relating to each. The *heart* includes our emotional self—our will, maturity, relationships, and feelings. It's also where we find joy and pleasure: expression, recreation, and leisure activities. *Soul,* meanwhile, involves our spiritual self. It encompasses worship and use of the sacraments, Bible study, prayer, observing Sabbath rest, and finding meaning and purpose in life. *Mind* involves our rational self: learning, wisdom, mental agility, challenges, thoughts, and beliefs. Finally, we have *strength.* Strength includes our physical self—energy, diet, exercise, rest, endurance, and resilience—as well as our talents and gifting.

What would it look like for you to care for yourself in each of these four dimensions? I can tell you this: When one of them is neglected or injured, the pain and symptoms will quickly seep into the others. Do you think it's a coincidence that people who neglect their physical wellness display pronounced unhappiness? Or how about the clarity of a person who neglects their spiritual dimension? Many nonbelievers I've met explain their lack of faith through rhetorical questions that *sound* reasonable and certainly carry emotional weight, "How could a loving God allow such horrible things to happen to people?" they ask. But when I probe a little deeper and ask them how they came to their conclusions, I almost always find pain, often from a neglected, seemingly unrelated dimension of their being. Something painful usually happened to them, and they didn't know how to interpret, process, or treat it. Soon, they became discouraged, sullen, and angry. Then, one day, they walked away from God or rejected him outright.

Equally true is that when we nourish one aspect of ourselves, the others benefit. You know how the body generates endorphins and feelings of well-being when you exercise? I love it when I get the "runner's high" and can suddenly push myself farther and longer. Or what about the deep sense of peace and rest you can project throughout the body through things like focused breathing and stretching? With benefits like these, it's no wonder you hear professional athletes describe their sports using phrases like "It's 80 percent mental" or "I'm playing on nothing but heart." They understand that competition involves one's mind, body, soul, and strength.

Let's not let life simply happen to us, since we have these powerful tools to empower ourselves for our daily callings intentionally. Instead, let's become the kind of people who tend diligently to our whole selves—heart, soul, mind, and strength. What if we attend and respond to our emotional lives, acknowledging them without being ruled by them? What if we become committed *disciples*—students in the kingdom of God, always seeking to align ourselves, understand his character, and serve others in loving response to a loving God? What if we fill our minds with wisdom, maturity, insight, and perspective? And above all, what if we fuel all of this with the abundance of energy we can tap into by becoming physically fit, well-fed, and well-rested?

After you rate yourself in each dimension, we move to the second part of empowerment: *building commitment.* Here, we discuss the reason you gave yourself these specific scores and where you'd like to see improvement. Some people tell me they want to improve in all four; others feel like they're only deficient in one. No matter where or how much you want to improve, you will need a rock-solid empowerment plan—and the commitment to see it through. You build commitment by tapping into your values, your goals, and a positive vision for yourself that pulls you rather than pushes you into the future. If you don't have the desire to change, nothing else will change either.

Next, we move to *building practice.* You could also think of it as the planning and execution phase of the empowerment plan. At this stage, you build a roadmap that steers you toward a *virtuous* cycle instead of a vicious one. Have you ever heard of the physics law that says, "Objects in motion tend to stay in motion unless acted on by a superior force?" This truism has a spiritual parallel: No matter which path you choose, you'll travel further in accordance with your choice and reap the rewards that go with it. You begin to integrate life-giving, energy-producing practices into your daily life. A big part of this section is developing SMART Goals (Specific, Measurable, Attainable, Relevant, Time-bound) to track and reflect on your progress. Some of these are unique to each area, while others will overlap. It is at this step that you learn to tap into your Divine GPS and create goals that are lasting and relevant to your core identity.

Building accountability is the fourth step of empowerment. Everyone needs support, encouragement, and accountability to put their plans into action. And everyone must find a unique way to hold themselves accountable to follow through on them. But let's face it—if we choose to go it alone, we'll come across moments when we feel like giving up. The time is *always* right to build close relationships with people who will be in your corner as your cheerleaders, who will encourage you and not let you throw in the towel just because you're tired or discouraged.

Remember, the biggest key to making changes in your life is consistency. If you think about it, you might already be consistent at being *inconsistent*. It's nothing to be ashamed of. Most people are that way. Wherever you're currently dissatisfied, you didn't get that way overnight. Let's take learning to walk. It takes months of crawling, standing, wobbling around, and gripping couch cushions and warm hands before we can do it on our own. And even when we know how to walk, we still have to learn how to run and jump without falling flat on our faces. In that learning process, we fail often. We fall down and get hurt, and then we try again. Too often, people want the process to be easy. They feel change should be effortless, like the flick of a light switch—a mere A/B decision in the mind. But in reality, it will be one of trial and error. It's okay to be patient with yourself and embrace failures! Failures are not meant to stop you in your tracks. If you pay attention, they can teach you a lot, either about what not to do or what to do differently.

In fact, one of the main reasons people don't feel empowered is a perceived lack of time. They think success is about going full-throttle all the time. We buy into this lie that we have to be super-human, that we need to do it all to have it all. (Good luck defining "it all.") This belief is simply not true; it actually leads to burnout.

Burnout is a massive roadblock to answering our calling in life. It stops us in our tracks and makes it feel impossible to get anything done. Many people experience burnout without being aware of it. Have you ever felt disconnected from your work or things you used to enjoy? Do you have trouble concentrating on simple tasks? Do you have an overwhelming sense of feeling under-appreciated or undervalued? Do you struggle to be thorough in your work? All of these things can be signs of burnout.

In order to avoid burnout, we need to establish a self-care routine. If you take anything from this chapter, please let it be this: *self-care isn't selfish.* As speaker Paul Scanlon says, "Your greatest gift to me is a healthy you."[1] It's a key ingredient to feeling sufficiently motivated in pursuit of our goals. But somehow, when we try to treat ourselves to a nice walk or an afternoon in the sun, we feel guilty and think of the more productive things we could be doing. We could be folding laundry or answering emails, but no! Instead, we're indulging ourselves. You have to risk prioritizing self-care, or you will eventually "feel the burn" of burnout.

From ancient times, the Judeo-Christian tradition placed a premium on the principle of Sabbath rest. The Israelites would divide farming property into seven plots, plant six of them, and let the seventh rest for one year before rotating. That way, each plot could rest for the following year. To produce good crops year after year, they learned that the land needed rest. There was a recognition that animals like horses and oxen also need rest. What is true about land and animals is also true about people. Observing the

---

1. Paul Scanlon (@paulscanlonuk), "Your greatest gift . . .," TikTok video, November 21, 2023, https://www.tiktok.com/@paulscanlonuk/video/7303851354735349025.

Sabbath honors the truth that human beings are no different from the rest of God's good creation. If rest was good enough for God after creating all things, what about you?

If you push yourself long enough and hard enough, eventually, you *have* to collapse or end up getting sick. We need to work from a place of rest, but far too often, the world rests from its place of work. The idea of working *from* rest, for me, means looking at Sunday as the beginning of the week rather than the end. This change of perspective means the first day of the week should be a day of rejuvenation where you take time to bask in God's goodness, trust in his provision, and celebrate the life and people surrounding you.

On an episode of my Called2B podcast, we talked about burnout with Pastor Kevin Scott.[2] Burnout, especially "Zoom burnout," accelerated enormously during the COVID-19 pandemic. When the country hit hard times, and the pandemic brought life as we knew it to a grinding halt, we leaned into work to help our economy stay afloat. With the transfer of work online, this often meant back-to-back meetings—all day, every day. But God did not make us to be machines. He made us to be human beings, and our bodies have ways of telling us to slow down and step back. Before we focus on our *doing*, we have to focus on our *being*. And that *being* needs rest.

Gallup® saw a massive spike in employee engagement during the pandemic. People were trying to handle the crisis and find better ways to work. But doing this without a method of replenishing yourself drains you, reducing your productivity. This reality was evident a few years later when engagement levels significantly decreased, and quiet quitting became a thing.

The business world *loves* productivity; especially for leaders in some companies, productivity is an idol. You would think we'd have learned by now that more doesn't necessarily equal better. But our compulsion keeps coming back to haunt us, which (I believe)

2. Travis Guse and Kevin Scott, "Dealing with Burnout (Episode 10)," Sep 7, 2022, in *Called2B Podcast*, YouTube video, produced by Kendall Guse, https://youtu.be/_8Xos5G53Wk?si=-LO5Hb63yOXk4grp.

is one reason God gave the commandment of keeping the Sabbath holy in the first place.

There will always be more to do and expectations to meet. But if you want to live and work within your calling, a hurried lifestyle will prove problematic. God doesn't like to have to shout, and he would prefer that we're internally driven to pursue him. (Yet, he has his ways of getting our attention, one way or another.) He's also promised us rest, life, and peace deep in our innermost being when we observe and honor the rhythms he built into creation. That is the sweet spot in life—confident, settled assurance from a well-rested, well-tended soul.

Of course, the idea of rest can be intimidating or overwhelming. You say *rest*, and people think you mean a three-month sabbatical. That's certainly *one* way to rest. (I highly recommend it if you can afford it.) But that's not the kind of rest I mean. We're talking about rest affordable for all, accessible to all. I've sometimes found when my tired soul thinks it needs two weeks off, that one simple afternoon is all that's required. I turn off the noise, go for a light stroll, or sit outside on the deck of my home. It's more than sufficient to recharge me.

Some people work in forty-five-minute sprints. Have you ever tried that? This idea is common among writers, but it can be applied to any work. You set a timer for forty-five minutes and tackle a project on your to-do list, giving it your full energy and attention. You don't answer your phone, browse the internet, or respond to emails. This forty-five minutes is focused and exclusive time. When the timer sounds, take a fifteen-minute break to go outside for a quick walk, smell the flowers, get something to eat, read a book, say a prayer, or whatever helps you recharge. Once that break ends, you set another forty-five-minute timer and dive back in or start the next project. You will be more effective if you take breaks! The harder you push without breaks, the less effective and creative you will be.

A friend of mine used to work hard as an insurance agent. He would go non-stop throughout the day. As time went by, he grew exhausted of this and formed a new habit—before he got out of his vehicle, anywhere he went, he would sit still for a few minutes. This time allowed space for him to breathe, think, prepare for the day, or pause and process events of the day before transitioning into the following action sequence of his day. This approach is beneficial if you're moving from one area of life, such as lifework, to another, like family.

I used to run for a track team in high school. When the season ended, I went from running every day to not running *at all*. The lack of physical exertion on my body put me in a foul mood. My grandma, whom I lived with at the time, grew weary of my bad attitude and told me to go for a run. I would come back from that run feeling better than I had in several days. It made me realize the importance of physical activity for my mental state. I've remained active ever since, mostly.

I didn't always know why I was upset, but I could tell my state of mind affected people around me. Give yourself the grace to say so if you don't feel "100 percent" in these moments. Too often, people ask how we are doing, and we respond reflexively with "good" instead of sharing how we truly feel. We don't have to do the journey of life alone. Telling others how you truly feel and what you are struggling with opens a door for them to help you find rest.

We marvel at celebrities, athletes, and politicians who hate their lives or can't handle the pressure that goes with them. They are the picture of what "success" looks like in our culture, yet they're *anything* but happy. What changed? What went wrong? It's never just *one* thing, but wouldn't you agree some of this is because of their non-stop lifestyles? Some of these people *never* get a chance to slow down and practice good self-care. Everywhere they turn, somebody wants something from them. There is a struggle between the balance of their public persona and their private life, and it's both risky and challenging to protect their time.

A professor once shared a great analogy for managing time. He brought out a jar and filled it with rocks. Rocks, he said, represent the important things in life: family, life goals, physical fitness, spiritual health, and financial stability. Important things need prioritizing—you don't want to neglect them. Then, he dumped a bunch of sand into the jar, filling the space around the rocks. The sand stood for the urgent things in life—your to-do list, emails in your inbox, other people's demands, etc. He talked about how vital it is to put in the essential things first (the rocks), or else the urgent things (the sand) will take up so much space that it becomes impossible to fit in the important ones. Then he cracked open a beer and poured it in, reminding the group to make some time for fun as well.

That example stayed with me. We can't pursue our callings if we're devoid of the empowerment we need. In the next section, we will discuss the steps to creating your empowerment plan. But remember, no plan will help if you're burned out. Include time in your plan to be still, regroup, and fill your cup. Even if time is in short supply, you can find it in the "micro." Everyone has sixty seconds here, ten minutes there, or a few hours now and then. Giving yourself those quiet moments to focus on your well-being each day will help you face the challenges ahead.

9

Creating Your Empowerment Plan

DAILY SCRIPTURE STUDY IS near and dear to my heart. It is a ritual that centers me. Many people start their days feeling like they're *behind*, as though the demands of life are already way ahead of them. I've felt that way many times, and to overcome it, my soul needed to hear the truth. Until I made studying God's word a daily nonnegotiable in my schedule, I would usually experience the sensation of "giving an inch" to chaos. It wasn't full-scale surrender, but little by little, chaos would chip away at my internal stability unless I thwarted it first. On one of those quiet, sunny mornings, as I read Luke 10:25–28 (ESV), my eyes were suddenly opened to something that I previously hadn't noticed.

> *And behold, a lawyer stood up to put him to the test, saying, "Teacher, what shall I do to inherit eternal life?" He said to him, "What is written in the Law? How do you read it?" And he answered, "You shall love the Lord your God with all your heart and with all your soul and with all your strength and with all your mind, and your neighbor as yourself."*

After all the years I spent reading those words, I couldn't believe how squarely they landed that day. Especially the words "heart," "soul," "mind," and "strength." Right there in that Scripture reading, the 4 Aspects of Self are mentioned. Our heart, soul, mind, and strength form the primary drivers of our physical and spiritual existence. While *identity* is the first step toward discovering our calling, now, the goal is to create a plan to level up our living it out. As we incorporate the 4 Aspects of Self into the *empowerment* phase of Called2B, we will build awareness, commitment, practice, and accountability in each of these areas.

And is it any wonder that Jesus followed up those four parts with the command to love our neighbors as ourselves? To me, this is confirmation that we're "blessed to be a blessing," as the old saying goes. First, we put in the investment to become empowered as believers, living out our callings, glorifying and loving God in the process. And right after that? Share it with somebody else.

BUILDING AWARENESS

It's easy sometimes to be like "spiritual bulimics," stuffing ourselves spiritually on Sunday and starving ourselves in our souls the rest of the week. The longer we go without hearing or reading the word, the more vulnerable we are to agreeing with half-truths and lies in our lives. Knowing our growth areas and addressing them in our schedules is vital to building awareness.

Below is a diagram of the 4 Aspects of the Self Wheel I developed. We'll use this tool in our first exercise. As we talked about in the previous section, each quadrant has to do with different aspects of our lives.

Give yourself a score based on your alignment in life in each section of the wheel. Self-scoring will be like scoring in golf: the lower the number, the better the score.

Do you feel strong in the heart quadrant? Do you enjoy good relationships, make time for self-care, and can you manage your emotions well? Then mark yourself as a one or a two in that quadrant. What about physical? Do you feel out of alignment? Do you wish you had more energy? Do you desire to run a marathon, even though you've never run a day in your life? Then mark yourself as an eight or a nine in that quadrant.

Empowerment Plan

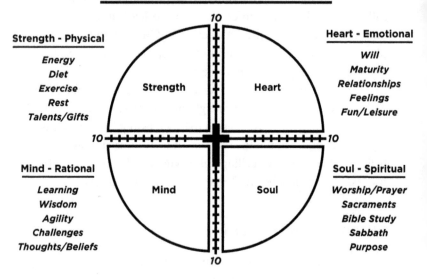

4 Aspects of Self Wheel

The goal of this exercise is to help you slow down and understand what is going on in your personal life. Think of it like stepping into a doctor's office. Before diagnoses or prescriptions, most doctors sit us down on a cold, sterile bed. They tap a hammer on our kneecap to test our reflexes. They put a cuff on our arm and check our blood pressure. They put a stethoscope on our chest and back to listen to our heart. They put a tongue depressor on our tongue and tell us, "Say 'Ah.'" Among medical professionals, these are known as "vital signs," which are obvious gauges that immediately indicate if something is out of whack with the human body.

After marking down all that information, the doctor begins to ask several questions. What is wrong? Where does it hurt? How long has this been happening? They dig deeper into the problem and potential causes of it in order to diagnose what ails you. This inquiry is the next level of assessment, beyond the vital signs, where complexity comes in.

Vital signs are common to all human beings. Once these questions begin, however, no two people are precisely the same. It would be great if doctors could say, "Just follow these five steps, and you'll be in perfect health." However, that would be absurd. People contract diseases, they inherit deficiencies, and they respond differently to certain stimuli and different environments. Some people have joint issues, while others may be in good health but accidentally hurt themselves. Some people get injured in athletics or health-promoting activities like exercise. Perhaps, for the worse, some people get sick or injured because of their own bad choices. And some are too embarrassed or uncomfortable to reveal the bad choices they made.

The 4 Aspects of the Self Wheel, like all the other tools in this book, is like going to the doctor—the more honest you are when you answer, the more accurately it can help you diagnose your overall well-being. If you're in poor condition, say emotionally or spiritually, don't be surprised if the road to recovery is more painful, the same way it is when you're in bad physical health. (Don't give up, either; commit to the recovery process!)

Once you have marked your score in each quadrant on the wheel, identify where you want to see change. Each of us has something unique to work on or perhaps several issues at once. A high or low score isn't necessarily good or bad. This score is simply an assessment, a snapshot of life as it currently stands today.

You may find these questions helpful when trying to identify change in regards to your well-being:

1. How satisfied are you with the scores in each quadrant? If you're not satisfied, why?

2. What would a one- or two-point positive change look like in this area of your life?

3. What can you do to effect this change, and what do you need to rely on God for?

Once you recognize where you want to change, you must make a commitment to follow through. This recognition brings us to the next step.

BUILDING COMMITMENT

Alan Deutschman wrote a fantastic book called *Change or Die*. In it, he details why *recognizing* the need for change isn't enough for it to take place. He shared an example of when physicians tell patients, "You need to change your lifestyle, or you will die." It doesn't work. In fact, doctors have found that telling patients "change or die" rarely creates lasting life changes. Instead, what *does* help change is to build a sense of commitment and desire to see change happen *within* the patient. It must be the patient who says, "I want to change."[1]

Motivation only lasts so long; it is a change in habits and *lifestyle* that produces what we're truly after. On the Called2B podcast, we have an episode titled "New Year, New You." During that conversation, we discussed the topic of New Year's resolutions and how they seldom last. Most resolutions have a shelf life of about two weeks.[2]

Business guru Peter Drucker has a good saying, widely attributed to him: "Culture eats strategy for breakfast." Any time you set your mind to change, the first obstacle is the *culture you brought with you*. Your life is not, nor has it ever been, random. You automatically bring existing habits, attitudes, and assumptions into anything you do. They may or may not have much impact on your day-to-day decisions. You might believe in leaving "everything up to chance." *But you've still made a choice that has consequences.* Companies looking to hire salespeople sometimes prefer inexperienced applicants because they know the applicants won't cling rigidly to how they were first taught to sell. This concept is a helpful

1. Alan Deutschman, *Change or Die* (New York: HarperCollins, 2007), 4.

2. Travis Guse, Trish Freshwater, and Kevin Scott, "New Year, New You (Episode 5)," Jan 12, 2022, in *Called2B Podcast*, YouTube video, produced by Kendall Guse, https://youtu.be/GoVPoOpUKIE?si=gKod61agUUdIx75K.

way to understand that, in the pursuit of growth, you will be your own biggest adversary. This reality is why we say that motivation can sustain you for a few weeks, but after that, real life takes over. That is when you'll be tested on your resolve to stay the course. So, your goal should be based on creating behavioral patterns that keep your habitual, older/former self off-balance.

Behavioral changes wield tremendous power to shape the world. At the time of this writing, many of my coaching clients are members of the youngest generations—Millennials and Generation Z. A few years back, the media reported an alarming trend that Millennials were avoiding home ownership and raising the question of whether owning a home would eventually become obsolete. Often cited was the fear of accumulating large amounts of debt, as previous generations had done. Since then, obviously, the younger generations have dispensed with the theory. But it goes to show—if you don't want debt, one way to avoid it is to change your habits and not buy a house! If you don't want to gain weight, you can always change how much you eat and the types of foods you consume. An entire field of science arose around behavioral therapy. This focus helps people create patterns of behavior to find more success in life, everyone from a successful CEO who recognizes a need for change in themselves to a child with autism so they can function better in the world around them.

A behavioral therapy book called *The Happiness Trap* by Russ Harris talks about how to make meaningful changes in your life. In a passage on commitment, Russ says: "Commitment, like acceptance, is a frequently misunderstood term. Commitment isn't about being perfect, always following through, or never going astray. Commitment means that when you do (inevitably) stumble or get off track, you pick yourself up, find your bearings, and carry on in the direction you want to go."[3]

Harris's quote can actually be validated through the study of neuroscience, where there is a law known as Hebb's Law: "Neurons that fire together wire together." The more we take specific actions,

3. Russ Harris, *The Happiness Trap* (Wollombi, NSW, Australia: Exisle, 2007), 256.

the more habits are formed, and the more we become a different person. In fact, the precise number of days to see an action become a habit in your life is sixty-six, or around two months.

To build commitment, identify the change you want in your life and determine how committed you are to making that change on a scale of one to ten. If you are at a seven or above, you are likely going to follow through. If you are at a six or below, you are less likely to succeed in the change you seek to make. It's at that point that you need to ask, "What would it take to change my commitment to a seven or higher?" My clients usually score seven to ten because they desperately recognize the need for change. But this isn't always the case. To troubleshoot your commitment to a goal, ask yourself these three questions:

1. What is the reason I'm not as committed to this goal as the others?

2. How aligned is this goal to my values and the changes I want to see in my life? Or is it something I feel *expected* to do, instead of something I want to do?

3. How can I change this goal to make a firm commitment? Do I need to make it smaller or adjust it so I have a better chance of hitting it?

Evaluate the motives behind your desired changes. Sometimes, we set goals for ourselves because we have been told all our lives we *should* be doing something. Forcing ourselves to take an action simply because someone repeatedly told us it is something we need to do *won't work*. In fact, these "goals" from the mouths of others may be totally unaligned with who we are at our core. That is why *identity* must come before *empowerment*.

In the next section, we will create goals. After you have them outlined, rate each one for your scale of commitment. You may find that some score less than others. If so, return to the questions above and adjust them until you aren't leaking energy on things you don't deeply desire to do.

BUILDING PRACTICE

The 4 Aspects of Self are not separate from each other. They overlap together because we are uniquely hybrid spiritual and physical creations of God. Positive changes we can make in one aspect of our lives can have beneficial results in other aspects.

In order to make your goals effective, I recommend smarting your goals up by creating SMART goals. Make them Specific, Measurable, Achievable, Relevant, and Time-bound. When our goals are specific, it means they are defined. The difference now is that your identity is *also* defined, which means the goal aligns with who you are in your being. It will still require effort and presents a level of difficulty, but you can overcome those when you sense *meaning* in what you're doing. The same goes for the measurability factor— it's like getting an A grade in your favorite class. You appreciate the content, you find value in learning, and you can attach performance markers because you sense the significance of your work.

Your goals will be more achievable this way. Who doesn't want to achieve more at something they can actually do? The relevancy factor will skyrocket in both the present and the future. And the power of time-bound goals, coupled with accountability, gives you a cutoff for completion and can add to your motivation. In coaching, asking a "when" question is where the rubber meets the road. It moves goal-setting from theoretical to reality. When you structure your objectives this way, you introduce a new version of yourself to the world—a person who says what they will do and then goes out and does exactly that. It's rarer than you might think. We're prone to get excited about change and jump in without thoroughly examining what it entails. Christ himself went on record to predict this and warn us against it.

> Suppose one of you wants to build a tower. Won't you first sit down and estimate the cost to see if you have enough money to complete it? For if you lay the foundation and are not able to finish it, everyone who sees it will ridicule you, saying, "This person began to build and wasn't able to finish." (Luke 14:28–30 NIV)

When you don't thoroughly think through a goal or you fail to understand the amount of time and energy it will take, you'll struggle to bring it to fruition. By doing the deep, thoughtful work ahead of time, you get a chance to adjust the goal. Sometimes, we make honest mistakes and suppose ourselves to be more capable than we actually are. It doesn't mean we can't do *anything*; it just means we must right-size our goals the way a skilled carpenter builds doorways, window sills, and stairwells suited to the square footage of the house he builds. Sort of like how Bob Wiley, played by Bill Murray, had to take "baby steps" in the movie *What About Bob?*

The best SMART goals contain one or more micro-goals you can complete quickly. Small wins do wonders for us from a neuroscience standpoint. When you achieve a goal, the brain releases dopamine, which promotes feelings of accomplishment, satisfaction, and well-being. Use this to your advantage and create micro-goals that allow you to tap into that reward center quickly. There's no harm in an extra boost of motivation every once in a while.

Another way you can tap into the reward center is by visualizing how you'll celebrate a goal once you've completed it. Little kids usually have someone there to say, "You did it!" or "Great job!" when they achieve something. I know we're all adults, but believe me, we don't stop needing this kind of encouragement as we grow older. Think of how you would celebrate a wedding, graduation, promotion, or winning a large account—and then right-size it to scale for the small wins. Dopamine may only last a short time, but that's all the more reason we should celebrate! Go out to dinner, take a day off, get a pedicure, or see a movie. Acknowledge and honor your victories, no matter how small they are, before it's too late to tell them apart from your losses.

Can you imagine standing at a grand cliff looking over a canyon? The drop below you is steep, opening up into a lush valley below covered in trees. A waterfall crashes next to you—the spray of the water dances across your face. Several miles down, it fills the river, snaking through the valley. The scent of the clean water and pine trees sweetens each breath you draw, and you hear the creatures of the forest chirping and chattering around you. You may wonder how anyone could fail to appreciate it, but rest assured, they do it all the time.

If we can walk by God's physical creation, say "huh," and then keep walking, how much more trouble do you think we'll have in appreciating our progress, which is frequently *in*visible? There is breathtaking beauty in our progress. It should not go ignored or unappreciated. Your hard work, just like the splendid view described, should be something you acknowledge. Otherwise, it begins to feel empty. And in the most painful of ironies, you are the person least likely to accept or recognize it! How sad when people who show wonderful signs of progress neglect to take time to celebrate their achievements.

It's now time to create some SMART goals. After completing the 4 Aspects of Self exercise, you likely have some thoughts on areas you want to change. Especially if you have asked yourself the question: "What would a one- or two-point positive change look like in this area?" It would help if you also intentionally set goals that include or engage your Gifts, Passions, and Strengths. I recommend creating one to three goals for each Aspects of the Self quadrant.

As you begin, here are a few helpful questions:

1. Name one or two small things you could do right now to make the biggest impact in each of these aspects of your life.

2. How could you leverage what is going well in one aspect of your life to help improve another one?

3. Name one SMART goal you could create for each aspect of your life in order to develop an empowerment plan.

4. What would it look like to merge several SMART goals into a more comprehensive well-being goal?

5. What obstacles or objections could get in the way of achieving these goals? How can you overcome this interference?

A word of caution. Be wary of what I call "gag" goals. These goals are so large that you gag thinking of what it would take to accomplish them. They often require achieving several steps (or smaller goals) before you can complete them. There are times and places for goals like these, but we're not there yet.

Instead, aim for goals that challenge you without getting so large that you feel overwhelmed. Your goals should feel more like a *gulp* than a gag. A "gulp" is much easier to swallow. The convenience store chain 7-Eleven actually sizes its soft drinks using this term. At my age, a "Gulp" is about all I can or should handle if I want to preserve my health. A "Big Gulp" is pushing it. (I always wanted Big Gulps as a kid, but my eyes were often bigger than my stomach.) A "Super Big Gulp" is totally out of the question, and a "Double Gulp" is probably more like a gag.

Gulps work in both negative and positive directions. Perhaps you're concerned that you won't see significant change if your goals aren't big enough. Let me assure you, that's not the case. Just as a 7-Eleven "Gulp" is more than enough soda for me, it also makes a great dosage of pure crystal mountain water, which is something I drink every day. I can feel the difference in my body's level of hydration and energy. That energy can then propel me to accomplish more.

BUILDING ACCOUNTABILITY

Now, it's time to find ways to hold yourself accountable to your goals. I'll stop here to recommend coaching, and for good reasons besides serving as a coach being part of my calling. Most people underestimate the *damage* they can do to themselves without accountability. You don't have to believe in God to know this—every time you pledge to do something and then fail to follow through, there *is* somebody watching and listening to you. Someone with huge control and influence over your life. Someone who records *every* word you say, every thought you think, and every action you take. Someone who is with you every waking (and sleeping) minute of every day of your life, right up until the moment you draw your very last breath. (Hint: It's not God, even though this is also true about him.)

It's YOU.

Your ears don't stop listening or tracking what you say simply because you open your mouth to state your intent to do something. They continue to listen, and they channel what you say back into your subconscious mind. This truth is one of the most unnoticed realities of life that leads to the experience we call "cognitive dissonance." It's one of the most significant sources of hypocrisy, and you can connect it to the depression and anxiety you feel when your identity isn't clear. Human beings don't do well when they're divided internally against themselves.

First, if you feel this way, God's grace and forgiveness abound for you each and every day. In Christ, you are a new creation; the old is gone, and behold, the new has come (2 Cor 5:17)! Remember, this is your new identity in Christ. Now, as a new creation, it is about finding someone who can help you be accountable in living out that new you and the new goals you have set for yourself. You *must* find a way to hold yourself accountable.

Among all the people you know, there's bound to be someone who cares about and encourages you—a friend, coworker, mentor, pastor, or parent. Show them your SMART goals and give them permission to hold you accountable. As an example, I know a writer whose goal was to write a book in a month. That's a challenge for anyone, but this young lady set daily word count goals, breaking down her writing into manageable chunks. Then she told two close friends, also authors, about this plan and asked them to hold her accountable. Every day, when she finished writing, she would share the amount of words she wrote with her friends in a group chat. They would congratulate and affirm her. If they didn't hear from her, they would ask how her word count was coming that day. On days when she struggled and wasn't able to get words on paper, she was able to confide in them and receive support, encouragement, and ideas to help her keep going.

Reporting our progress to the people we care about causes something interesting to happen. Their support and encouragement have a way of egging us on toward the finish line. We don't want to disappoint them. This kind of encouragement is the power of creating a support system. If you start to slip or stray from the goal, you can talk to your supporters about it. Their feedback reminds you of what you set out to achieve. They bring you back to your "why," as Simon Sinek would say. If need be, they can even bring you back further to the "who" of your identity. You set out to become someone *different* from who you were, and the people who hold you accountable bear witness. There's no turning back now.

Your empowerment plan is starting to take shape. The SMART goals you created may overlap or have an overarching theme (which will enhance how you execute them). If you find you have similar goals, ask yourself how you can condense them. Consider creating, perhaps, a "happy hour" in your day.

What does this look like practically? One of my coaching clients, Gene, for example, struggled with anger. One of the goals he set for himself to address his anger was to take long walks during his "happy hour" daily, which also benefited his body (strength). On these long walks, he would engage his mind by thinking through what was truly important and how he wanted to show up in stressful situations. In addition, he would pray during these walks, lifting up his frustrations to God, thus benefiting his soul. After his walks, he met up with some friends at a local coffee shop, which helped to nurture his heart. Together, they would have a devotion which tended his soul. From Gene's empowerment plan concerning one aspect of himself, his heart, he was able to improve his overall well-being as the other aspects of his self also reaped the benefits through this "happy hour."

Creating an empowerment plan to improve your well-being while including all your SMART goals can be challenging. You're looking inwardly at parts of yourself you may not have observed before. You're discovering things you want to change. It can be emotional and provoke critical thoughts like "Why am I this way?" or "I can't do this." These emotions are natural and normal, but you must resist the temptation to let them overwhelm you. Give yourself some grace because God's grace for you in Christ knows no bounds. And if you need to, find someone to help you process what you're feeling.

Here are a few things to look out for. If your goals feel paralyzing, like slogging through mud, it's time to reevaluate and think through the empowerment plan.

Resistance is a natural and normal feeling when trying to complete challenging goals, but paralysis usually means you are overwhelmed. It's a sign to adjust and tap into your natural strengths to find a more motivating goal.

Empowerment Plan

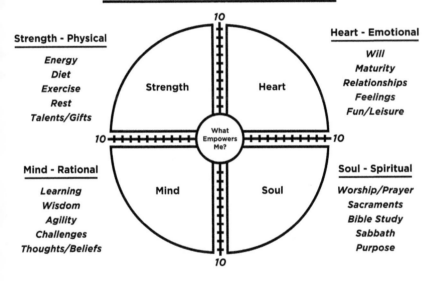

A word of caution, however: not *everything* can be bypassed because it's outside your zone of genius. Perhaps you find basic physical hygiene to be tedious. It doesn't mean you should stop doing it, and you can't outsource it to someone else. In every area of your life, there will always be things only you can do for yourself, whether you happen to enjoy them or not. We're not talking about those things here.

You now have a set of goals to help align yourself with who you want to become for the sake of loving and serving others. God calls us to use what he's given us, and this empowerment plan helps you find the best ways to do that. Please note that plans do change over time. No one can know for sure if this plan will stay the same for your entire life. You should plan to periodically assess if your empowerment goals are still the right ones. It's okay to change them. Growth in our lives brings us to new levels of passion, hopes, and dreams. Make sure your goals connect to those changes when they happen.

This journey will take dedication and energy. You may not get it right every day. But it will be well worth it in the end.

10

Making an Impact

THE THIRD ELEMENT IN the Called2B vocational coaching framework is *impact*. To make a greater impact with the Gifts, Passions,
and Strengths that God has given us, it is sometimes necessary to
make a profound change in our lives.

This principle was the case with Jason. In many ways, Jason
was going through the motions in both his personal and professional life, pretending to be what others expected of him without
ever truly knowing himself. After losing his first pastoral call for
not being what his congregation expected, and then stepping away
from his next congregation as his marriage fell apart, Jason felt he
had no value in the life of the church and eventually shirked away
from reentering ministry afterward. But even after finding other
work, Jason fought to stay engaged and felt exhausted when he
came home every day. He wanted to be more fulfilled in his day-
to-day work but wasn't sure what that would entail after so much
had happened inside and outside of himself.

To pursue his next chapter of life, he returned to school and
committed himself to study. Jason focused on a degree in community development and graduated after a few years of diligent

work, even while teaching grade school full-time. Unfortunately, as he neared the end of his coursework, he became increasingly uncertain how his new degree could translate into job prospects. Making the impact he believed God wanted him to make seemed to grow further and further out of reach. Nobody was hiring for his unique combination of expertise. He knew he wanted to pursue his passions, but a shortage of openings made it difficult.

Through the Called2B assessments and follow-up coaching conversations, we uncovered the types of change Jason wanted to see in his life. We determined how his new training and Divine GPS could best be used and strategized about *where* he could offer them. Yet, as we did, we found that there wasn't a specific organization that served these needs within his geographical area.

So, Jason decided to start his own "enterprise." Not a business, mind you, but definitely an enterprise from a kingdom perspective. He ended up in a role with Harris County in Houston, working in community development and affordable housing. Together, we brainstormed the elements of how he could influence people to think outside the box beyond their own immediate self-interest to love and serve their community. In addition to his day job, he also found opportunities to do pastoral work with a local congregation, helping them look beyond the walls of their ministry to be a greater blessing in their own community. Today, he makes frequent, substantial changes in the lives of people within the communities he works in.

Living out our ultimate identity in Christ through our unique identity, according to God's workmanship, enables us to make a more significant impact in the world around us. We do so by using our Divine GPS identified through the Called2B coaching framework and leveraging this God-given design to serve others in relevant and transformative ways. In the horizontal callings of life, it is all about "loving your neighbor," just as Jesus calls us to do as his followers. This calling is the pathway to finding more meaning and fulfillment in our daily lives.

Impact doesn't have to be something big. You don't have to change your job or do something tremendously costly or

extravagant. It's about finding a place in the world where your empowered identity reflects the kingdom of God in your day-to-day
interactions with others. As Frederick Buechner would say, it's "the
place where your deep gladness and the world's deep hunger meet."[1]

American culture teaches that success is meant to be big,
even "super-sized." I don't know about you, but I get exhausted just
thinking about it. Why should we put ourselves through those motions when we can celebrate and enjoy success that's much more
widely accessible?

In the tradition of Martin Luther, there are two distinct cat-
egories for thinking about God: the Theology of Glory and the
Theology of the Cross. In the Theology of Glory, you might expect
God to show up in large-scale, historic, and unprecedented events.
In fact, from time to time, he is present in the spectacular and in
things we might deem successful. Things like parting the Red Sea
or Jesus healing a leper are grand events that make his existence
plain to all who have eyes to see and ears to hear. They are large,
eye-catching, and unforgettable. You can point to them and be certain they happened because he willed them to happen.

However, in the Theology of the Cross, God is found in the
small and lowly things—including hurt, loss, and brokenness. It's
not about *how* Jesus is glorified but *where* he is glorified. And where
and how is Jesus glorified most clearly? He is found on the cross at
Calvary, lifted high as the Lamb of God who takes away the sins of
the world. There, Jesus is revealed as a Suffering Servant from Isa 53
who was despised and rejected to bring healing to the world. The
best part of this kind of glory is that there's so much more of it to
go around. Whether it's the loss of a friend, our own guilt, pain, or
anger, it's what drives us to him and where he meets us the most.
The book of Hebrews tells us, "For we do not have a high priest who
is unable to sympathize with our weaknesses, but one who in every
respect has been tempted as we are, yet without sin" (Heb 4:15 ESV).

Impact, like the Theology of the Cross, is where we, as followers of Christ, deny ourselves, take up our crosses, and follow him.

1. Frederick Buechner, *Wishful Thinking* (San Francisco: Harper & Row,
1973), 95.

Each person carries their own cross—some to slums in Third World countries, others to corporate boardrooms. As we seek to love and serve, we will discover the "dark side" of even the brightest, most exciting, and holiest callings. We will fail, we will face the unknown, and we will encounter challenging realities we didn't expect.

The cross of our callings is where we find life and new beginnings. You can see it in those moments when we experience failure and come to the end of ourselves. It is there we have nowhere to turn but the foot of the cross, where Jesus meets us with grace, forgiveness, and a new beginning rather than with condemnation. It is there, at the cross, that the Spirit of God not only refreshes us but shows up with fresh expressions of his moving in and through our callings in life.

Now, even with the tools I give you here, you should expect *partiality*. That's the nature of things. You will have times of despair and moments of self-doubt. There is no recipe for a perfect life this side of eternity. The point of Called2B is to experience more while being content without "having it *all*." That only comes later, on the other side of our last breath.

The cross we bear every day in our callings is bound together with the path we choose. When we seek to offer our talents in the service of others, we should be prepared for a real-life version of the classic board game "Chutes and Ladders." Remember that game? First, you make progress. Then you hit a roadblock and slide backwards by several squares and, at times, even all the way back to the beginning again. This game reminds us that there are ups and downs in all of our callings. Even in the down times, God's grace is where Jesus meets you, and what matters most is that, by his strength, you are still in the game we call life. The further ahead you get, however, the more clearly you can reassess your empowered identity as you prepare to continue until that day we are called to glory.

When you search for a setting to make an impact, start in the places where you already have a deep reach. Most people want to start off in the deep end, with "millions of followers" or a powerful, socially prominent position. But when you're first starting, you have no connection to these people. So, why not begin with the people in your house, your church, your school, your workplace, or your immediate community?

This approach was the case with Heidi, who was a member of a church I served previously. She sang with the praise team, helping lead worship, and truly enjoyed serving God in this way. However, at that time, Heidi felt that the impact she was making for Jesus was limited by what she did within the congregation. When I began my coaching journey, I offered to coach Heidi through ways for her to make a greater kingdom impact in every aspect of her life. She discovered that through her work as the alumni and development director at a local university, she was able to influence and serve with greater intentionality those she encountered daily in her work. Over time, as she loved and served those in her sphere of influence, that sphere began to grow. Eventually, she was asked to become the chair of the local Chamber of Commerce, a role that she would not have even considered just a few years prior. Heidi became an invaluable resource in her community, and this, too, was as much of a holy calling as her service within her church.

The best definition I've ever heard of what it means to have a calling in life is "As far as our eyes can see, and as far as our hands can reach—that is your calling today." Your calling is to love and serve the people God places in your sphere of influence every day. We are called to do something, not *everything*. Be willing to start small and let God expand your impact.

When I was young, I used to sell shoes for Nike. One of my brothers is a garbage collector, while another owns a business pouring concrete. These jobs may seem small, mundane, and unimportant and, perhaps to some, these kinds of work are beneath them. But through the eyes of faith, you'll see these are also holy callings. God *is* concerned about the feet of children and adults. God *does* care about our hygiene and sanitation. (Would he have spent that much time teaching Moses about it if he didn't? Imagine our world without organized trash collection!) It's a good thing we have clean streets and smooth paths to walk on, where we don't have to worry about stepping in holes or getting hit by cars.

There is a considerable percentage of young people today, in particular, who desire fame and fortune. Many who participate in sports want a career as a professional athlete. While these dreams are exciting, they are *extremely* difficult and competitive to attain. Instead, if you want to know where you can create the most impact, you should first look to *who* God has created and redeemed you to be. There are plenty of successful athletes, entertainers, and leaders outside Hollywood, the major leagues, and national capitals. God may indeed call you to one of these places, but those calls frequently arrive as doors *he opens* rather than ones you can open and enter on your own.

Once you're clear on your calling—who you are in Christ and how he's gifted you—it's time to look for opportunities to spread your influence. Scripture is abundantly clear: if we are faithful with small things, we can also be entrusted with big things (Luke 16:10). You love and serve where you can, how you can, until God decides to grow your sphere of influence. This calling may feel too small, but you need to work your way up. You need practice—the law of ten thousand hours, as Malcolm Gladwell would say. You are a student of impact today. You need to add knowledge, skill, and experience to your Divine GPS. But if you work diligently and make an impact in the lives of more and more people, you will find your reputation and influence *spreading*.

Additionally, your calling will require you to work with others. Returning to your Divine GPS, a strength isn't truly a strength until we partner with somebody who has complementary talents to our own. This reality is the power of two, as we hear about in Eccl 4:9 (NIV), for "two are better than one, because they have a good return for their labor." We are called to be in partnership and community with others. Be the part you are supposed to be, *and* partner with others who make up for what is lacking in you so God can have the greatest impact through more than one channel. It isn't solely about what you are doing but what God can do through you in partnership with others. Let's take a look at Jesus' disciples. He never sent them out alone. He sent them out in pairs, and they carried his message together. You will find more success if you build a community to support you as you pursue your calling.

On another Called2B podcast entitled "Living Your Calling," we discussed how living an impactful life touches the people you help directly, and through them, you also touch the people *they* impact in the process.[2] The ripple effect starts with you. A friend of mine from England and I ran cross-country together at Boise State University. First, God used me to help bring him to faith. Amazingly, he was a much more effective evangelist for the gospel than I ever was, talking with everyone about his faith in Christ in a winsome way. Part of loving and serving others is passing on what we learn and inspiring them to pursue their own calling. It's easy to get caught up in individual stories and contests over who has more money, possessions, or prestige. If we're going to worry about numbers and tallies, let's focus on how many people we can impact and spur them on to their own greatness in God's economy.

As Jesus said in Matt 5:14–16 (NIV), "You are the light of the world. . . . In the same way, let your light shine before others, that they may see your good deeds and glorify your Father in heaven." Our primary purpose in life is to reflect God to the world and to reflect creation back to God in all of our callings. How do you do that? You do that by utilizing the best that God has gifted to you in your Divine GPS in love and service to those he has placed before you in your various responsibilities in life.

Finding purpose can bring comfort, especially when it comes to finding meaning and a sense of significance in life. What if you aren't sure how to achieve it? Our calling doesn't have to be "big," nor do we need personal requests from God on stone tablets. It can begin small, and it can even *stay* small. Stop thinking "the American way," and start thinking of your true purpose from a kingdom perspective. Think about engaging with a child as you teach them to eat independently. They struggle to scoop with a spoon by moving it too quickly or at the wrong angle, and the food falls off. They become frustrated and irritable. So, as the parent, you take the time to sit with them patiently. You show them how

---

2. Travis Guse and Kevin Scott, ft. Rob Brown, "Living Your Calling (Episode 8)," Apr 20, 2022, in *Called2B Podcast*, YouTube video, produced by Kendall Guse, https://youtu.be/wsZzDssmNoo?si=ZoWCB8LKY3vDahrM.

to hold the spoon, how to bring it to their lips, and how to control it so the food doesn't fall off. They may take some time to learn, but with your persistence, patience, and compassion, you and they will eventually succeed.

That is impact.

Another example is a sales associate training another. During a difficult day for the new associate, they experience multiple rejections. You sit down with them and work through their pitch together. You take time to point out where they become too pushy or fail to ask the right questions. You show them how to stand, the gestures to use, and you reassure them throughout the process. Your strengths of determination and communication bring about success to the people you influence.

That is impact.

I once worked with a young man who had difficulty relating to many people in our congregation. I noticed his anger and could sense how it affected him and the people around him. He enjoyed pushing buttons and being something of a nuisance to others. Rather than avoiding or ostracizing him, I made a point of speaking with and getting to know him. I showed patience and took an interest in what he had to say. With God's strength, I did my best to reflect the love Jesus had revealed to me in his life as well. I never actually coached or mentored him in the formal sense. I simply and consistently displayed interest and concern for his life. Years later, unprompted by any particular event, that same young man approached me with a young family in tow and said, "Thank you for the investment you made in my life."

That is impact.

Impact is hard to measure. Unless people reveal how much you have helped them, the true impact of your investment in their life is anybody's guess, and it is frequently difficult to quantify this side of eternity. But that's all the more reason you should do it. You've been promised a day in the kingdom where you will enjoy the company of all those whom you have impacted in this earthly life for eternity. What a joyous day that will be!

11

How Do You Make an Impact?

IN THIS SECTION OF Called2B, we'll examine how God has wired you to make a greater *impact* in your love and service to others in your various areas of responsibility in life. You will discover how he's gifted you and the passions he has set within you. This examination delves into what burdens your heart or what concerns you may have for the world. This step is where we ask ourselves, "Who needs what I have to offer?" We are called to serve in many general ways, but our specific service is where we can make the most significant impact with our God-given talents.

When it comes to figuring out how to help others, I used to tell my coaching clients to ask themselves, "What does the world need?" But this question is too broad with too many variables. It's overwhelming, like trying to figure out where the best place is to put a drop of water in the Sahara Desert, hoping to bring life. Instead, as you go through these exercises, ask yourself, "Who needs what I uniquely have to offer?"

"Seth Godin wrote a book a number of years ago called *Tribes*, which explains where your sphere of influence is and how to find people who need what you offer. It focuses on how you can be a servant leader and make the greatest impact with people who are yearning for leadership and connection. In other words, you will make the greatest impact when you "find those who need what you have to offer, and serve them."[1] There are plenty of places you fit. These positions are all around us, hiding in plain sight, unnoticed or unknown. It doesn't mean they're not there or that we shouldn't bother looking for them. Life can sometimes feel monotonous, as though the same people, places, and limited opportunities for years on end box you in. I would argue the opposite: the familiarity of our surroundings *conceals* what has changed so that we have to pay a little more attention than usual to find the "gold."

Getting to this "gold," particularly with help from a coach, requires you to dig deep. There are *investments* involved—spiritual, emotional, and even sometimes financial. But the most significant investment you'll make is time. Sometimes, I work with clients one hour per week for twelve coaching sessions. Occasionally, we have a longer coaching journey together—as much as twenty-four weeks in a row. We resist our tendency to look for quick fixes (cookie cutter, assembly line, mass-produced solutions that only add to the confusion). Your unique calling cannot be mass-produced. It takes investing in yourself and hard work, and you'll have to risk stepping beyond your comfort zone. However, the rewards are lasting fulfillment, meaningful connections, and uplifting relationships.

My coachees go on to do what they do and achieve their impact because they have a deeper awareness of who they are in Christ, how they have been gifted, and the passions God has laid on their hearts. As a result, they often find fulfillment and a sense of purpose in making a difference.

Others who work with me as a coach aren't aware of the abundance of opportunity around them. With some coaching help, they learn to see those opportunities everywhere. We sometimes go through life with blinders on, which obscures our vision. It's time to open them up to see a larger vision of the difference you can make so you can go through life with greater intentionality.

---

1. Seth Godin, *Tribes* (New York: Penguin, 2008), 8.

There's no more confusion over who you are versus who you're not or what God has gifted you with the ability to do.

I know a young woman who got laid off from a lucrative and long sales career. It was comfortable and familiar. As she searched for a new job, she received an invitation from the company where her husband worked. They were *adamant* that she would be wonderful in an HR manager position with them. They showered her with praise for her professionalism and empathy for others, insisting she'd fit the role, even with no previous experience.

It filled my heart with joy to hear her describe how she turned down the offer. She knew her strengths and weaknesses and understood herself enough to know that this role was way off-base. Was it steady work with a good company and an employer chomping at the bit to hire? Absolutely! However, she held steady and gently refused the offer. It wasn't about being good enough to do well in the role. She wanted to make an *impact*, and she knew it wouldn't come with "good enough." She had to find where she could make the greatest difference.

When we gain an understanding of our strengths, we can use them more intentionally and to great effect. If you know your strength is communication, communicate more. If your strength is being strategic, you can offer help making plans as often as you want. There's a beautiful, free-flowing nature to helping people where you're naturally strong. It's like having Celine Dion offer to sing with you, or Elton John play the piano. Whereas this young woman knew she might possess the *skill* for the job, she was free to turn it down because it didn't align with her Divine GPS. That gave her the liberty to pursue a full-time activity that fit deeply into her God-given design and allowed her to better serve the world around her.

I want you to experience this kind of impact. In the next section, we'll proceed with some exercises to discern how you can do just that. You'll learn how to use the "Basic Calling Model," which I've modified, and the "BLESS" model to love and serve your neighbors with greater kingdom impact through your various callings in life. By the end of this exercise, you can expect some

concrete examples of who you should seek out, where to go, what
to do, how to do it, and why.

12

How Do You Make a Difference?

A FEW YEARS AGO, I visited one of my favorite local coffee shops. The manager who worked there learned I was a Gallup® Strengths Coach and told me excitedly about how she was using the assessment.

"That's cool you're a coach!" she said. "Each of us on the team took the CliftonStrengths Assessment. We keep trying to retake it in order to get the results of the star regional manager. We all want to be more like him!"

Her response caught me by surprise. As she handed me my latte, I said, "You know, it's meant to tell you what YOUR strengths are in life. You will become a star manager much faster if you use your own strengths to do so."

This manager's philosophy seems to be very prevalent in our culture: "Just find out what successful people do, copy it, and you too can be successful!" That may sound simple, especially if the work is already cut out for you. But here's the truth: there is *no* secret sauce to effective leadership. No shortcut. There's no magic spell, and there's no "guru" who's doing everything right. It's a trap to look for the "silver bullet." It is not about trying to be like somebody who is doing it better than you; it's about being who God has created and redeemed you to be! You are most effective when you leverage the Gifts, Passions, and Strengths that God has placed inside of you. The most direct route to success lies in knowing where to serve, with whom, and how God's workmanship in your life can contribute to you being an authentic servant-leader.

Some people are prone to jealousy, even hatred, when they see others who have not only found what they are good at but also how to fit it into their everyday life. This reality is a bitter pill to swallow, especially if we feel lost or uncertain of where to go next. In the movie *Amadeus*, one of the main characters is a composer named Salieri in the court of Austria. His career is going smoothly until he meets a young Wolfgang Amadeus Mozart. Mozart's prodigious musical talent wows everyone in Vienna, but Salieri grows bitter and resentful, infuriated at God for giving Mozart such gifts.

"From now on, we are enemies," Salieri hisses at God in his private chamber. "Because you have chosen for your instrument a boastful, lustful, infantile, smutty little boy . . . and given me for reward only the ability to recognize the incarnation."[1] This perspective of being spiteful of someone else's strengths is not a healthy way to deal with your own weaknesses.

God created each one of us uniquely. We're custom-built, designed, and gifted for a purpose he had in mind before we were born. In Ps 139:13–16 (ESV), we hear:

> For you formed my inward parts; you knitted me together in my mother's womb. I praise you, for I am fearfully and wonderfully made. Wonderful are your works; my soul knows it well. My frame was not hidden from you, when I was being made in secret, intricately woven in the depths of the earth. Your eyes saw my unformed substance; in your book were written, every one of them, the days that were formed for me, when as of yet there was none of them.

1. Milos Forman, dir., *Amadeus*, Orion Pictures, Prague and Kroměříž, 1984, DVD.

God doesn't do cookie-cutter or assembly-line human beings. Humans might create products in an assembly line, but he doesn't do it that way.

Can you imagine if everything you made was a masterpiece? No, neither can I. But God can, and God does. Your thoughts, feelings, emotions, hopes, wishes, and dreams are unlike any other. They come from a unique life experience and set of relationships. In his book *The Dictionary of Obscure Sorrows*, John Koenig describes the word *sonder*. Sonder is the realization that each random passerby lives a life as vivid and complex as your own.[2] Most people give this concept barely a passing thought, but when it comes to our calling in life, we need to use it every day. You and I need constant reminders that we are masterpieces, unique from the rest. Your path to a meaningful and impactful life will be fresh and uncharted; it will not be the same as mine.

Step one is to find where your calling fits. From there, the path to *impact* will wind and turn. It may double back or come to dead ends (where you must retrace your steps). Your secure identity in Christ will brace you to handle the surprises that crop up along the journey.

Another illusory trap to avoid pursuing is something called a "*kairos* moment." These moments are when somebody like Bill Gates is in precisely the right place, with the right idea, at the right time, when an entire revolutionary age is waiting to burst. These moments are unique, unusual, and can take a lifetime to reach (or they may never happen in your lifetime). As we pass through life, we may find ourselves with the right idea, but we're way ahead of our time. Or we might have an excellent idea, and we're too late; someone else has already bought the domain. Moments like these are beyond even the people who take advantage of them. Bill Gates (or Steve Jobs, Mark Zuckerberg, or Elon Musk) are anomalies. It is not the wisest to spend your energy chasing the kind of global success they've had.

2. John Koenig, *Dictionary of Obscure Sorrows* (New York: Simon and Schuster, 2021), 123.

Kairos moments are of divine design. Outcomes are always in God's hands. We've spent centuries trying to take matters into our own hands to create them, to no avail. However, we can control our preparedness to adapt to the way the world changes around us. We can pray, watch for, and be ready to step into a *kairos* moment if and when God opens the door for us. Recently, I heard the word *luck* defined as the moment when preparation meets opportunity. I would define that instead as a *kairos* moment.

The first tool to help you make a more impactful difference through your various callings in life is the Basic Calling Model. I adapted this coaching tool to help you process how you can aim your Divine GPS in service to others. I looked high and low for the original creator of this tool, as it's important for me to acknowledge and give the appropriate credit, but I could not find the creator. If you, dear reader, happen to recognize it while reading this book and can tell me, please reach out! I would love to meet this individual and hear more about where this model came from.

Basic Calling Model

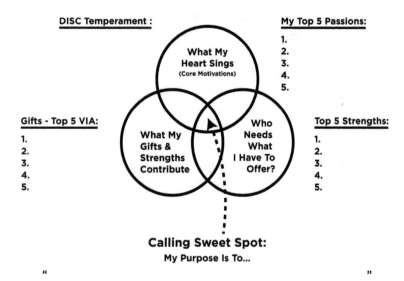

DISC Temperament :

My Top 5 Passions:
1.
2.
3.
4.
5.

What My Heart Sings
(Core Motivations)

Gifts - Top 5 VIA:
1.
2.
3.
4.
5.

What My Gifts & Strengths Contribute

Who Needs What I Have To Offer?

Top 5 Strengths:
1.
2.
3.
4.
5.

Calling Sweet Spot:
My Purpose Is To...

"   "

The first circle represents how the Gifts of your personality (temperament and character) and Strengths (talents) contribute. The second circle is what makes your heart sing—your Passions in life (interests and concerns). The third circle contains the question, "Who needs what I have to offer?" This third circle is where you should look at who your neighbors are in the four domains of life (Family, Church, Lifework, and Society) to see who you directly influence.

At the intersection of these three circles, we can, at last, discern our "Calling Sweet Spot," that place where we can have the greatest impact. Nothing is better than hitting the sweet spot when a driver strikes the ball off the tee in a game of golf! And there is nothing better than hitting that sweet spot in living out your calling! It looks different for each person, depending on your Divine GPS and who figures strongest in your circle of influence. The more aligned these three circles become, the larger the sweet spot of your calling grows—and the greater your chances of profoundly impacting others. More than any other, this model helps you discern your purpose or your "why" in life.

Author and speaker Simon Sinek is famous for his book *Start With Why*, which teaches people to do work that inspires them. He talks about how to find your "why" and apply it to your daily life. Our "why" is what motivates us, even on the darkest days. It doesn't mean we take world-changing action each day, but we know why we do what we do. We find renewal in it consistently and carry it through hills and valleys as fuel for the journey.[3]

Colorblind artist Rob Moore joined us for the Called2B podcast and shared how he paints. He also disclosed how he discovered the secret of turning his *limitation* into his "why" through his art. Using both hands simultaneously, Rob takes the three primary colors (red, yellow, and blue) and combines them into extraordinary masterpieces. He uses a few specific components, and with a master's hand, he creates something unique, memorable, and beautiful.[4]

3. Simon Sinek et al., *Find Your Why* (New York: Portfolio, 2017), 4.

4. Travis Guse and Trish Freshwater, ft. Rob Moore, "Everyday Believers—Created to Create," Oct 19, 2021, in *Called2B Podcast*, YouTube video, produced by Kendall Guse, https://youtu.be/5hOGIw7_esg?si=xzGt3uoYI_NTp15Y.

Rob's approach to painting is similar to discovering our unique sweet spot. We have the three basic components of discerning your calling (like three primary colors), but how these get painted together is unique to each person. Discovering your calling is not a paint-by-numbers creation! It's custom, guided by the Master's (God's) hand. (And our Master knows his "why.")

The following coaching tool is the BLESS© model. BLESS, which stands for "bond, learn, engage, serve, and share," is part of a larger body of work called iNeighborhood, developed by Bruce Jaeger for the Southeastern District (LCMS). I have been given permission to utilize the BLESS model with my Called2B coaching framework.

The BLESS model gives you some key steps to think about as you work to develop trust among those you are called to love and serve in your different stations of life. To leverage your "Calling Sweet Spot" and impact the people in your world, you may need a strategy to first *bond* with them.

To truly serve people, we need to know them beneath the surface. We make assumptions about people all the time without taking the time to understand them truly. The best relationships I've ever had are the ones where I take time to get to know the other person. Similarly, the worst relationships were those where I chose to remain in the shallow end, making judgments and assumptions without any context or depth.

For example, I knew of a volunteer group that went to an impoverished country and built a medical facility for a local community. This community struggled with frequent, widespread sickness. The solution seemed simple: they needed better medical care. However, the hospital didn't solve the problem; the community members continued to get sick.

A second volunteer group went to the same village and saw that the hospital *was* being highly used. After establishing a bond with the tribe, the volunteers discovered that this group of villagers couldn't access clean drinking water. So, the second group of volunteers worked to improve the drinking water and, suddenly, the medical center wasn't quite as busy as before.

The first group assumed one thing; the second group took the time to get to know the actual needs of those within this community. Both were well-intentioned, but only one truly made a lasting change for everyone concerned. We need to do the same due diligence when offering our Gifts, Passions, and Strengths in service to others in all the areas of responsibility in our lives. Sometimes, getting to the root of the issue requires a deliberate time of bonding with those we seek to bless.

Developing trust doesn't often come quickly or easily. It comes with friendship, shared experiences, reminiscing on memories, and consistently being present in someone's life. It means being the first one to reach out or check in if they are sick. You cannot become a confidant or trusted friend if you do not first find ways to build a bond.

Stephanie, my wife of over thirty years, is not only a confidante but also a complementary partner in life. She has a wonderfully logical and analytical personality, which proves extremely helpful to someone like me. Because of the bond between us and how well we understand each other, I can tell her about my latest idea, and Stephanie helps me analyze what's realistic about it versus what is over the top. I'd have long since thrown myself overboard if she wasn't such a dependable anchor.

This example of my wife leads us to the following attribute in the BLESS model—*learn.* Seek to understand another person's story, their gifts and talents, their hopes and dreams, as well as their hurts and failures in life. This discovery often happens along the way of life while becoming friends and developing a relationship. "Bond" and "learn" are closely aligned. Yet learning does take it one step further: You must be willing to sit with them through discomfort. Walk them through the struggles they face and the fears they must overcome. Help them remember their goals and dreams as they seek a better future for their lives.

After bonding and learning, we must intentionally *engage* in life with people. Be present with them and honor their condition, moment by moment. Take time to help in ways that communicate your affection and appreciation for them. This type of engagement with others may sound challenging with how busy we are in our daily lives. It means we need to be intentional about where we spend our time. It may mean saying "no" to some really good things in life so that we can say "yes" to the people God calls us to love and serve.

And as we do, we need to pay attention to the limitations of our own souls when it comes to our engagement. You should be able to sense this by weighing your physiological and spiritual reactions against the number of people you know and interact with on a daily basis. If it feels like a stretch to nurture good relationships you've already built, you may need to lighten your overall intake. Some people have the CliftonStrengths® talent theme of "Woo®," allowing them to handle many relationships simultaneously. Others are "Relators®," meaning they prefer to go deep relationally with only a few people.[5] We each have a different relational capacity.

A useful analogy for understanding this idea of relational capacity is Legos, the children's toy building blocks. We have *tubs* of them in our house from when our son was younger, now in preparation for future grandchildren. Some Lego pieces have two studs, some have four, some have eight, and some have many more. As I look at them, I realize how well they represent the connection points between human beings. We each have a different capacity for connections with others. Some people are introverted and have just a few connection points, while others are extroverts who can handle more. If your relational capacity is all taken up with work (or even involvement in your church) and you have no energy or time for others, you can't connect with *anyone*—let alone anyone new. Sometimes, you have to free up some of this capacity to more fully engage with your existing tribe or perhaps new people in your life.

After you engage, you should find ways to *serve*. Here is where we understand someone else's needs and struggles. It's now our turn to apply our Divine GPS. By this time, you should have identified a struggle you may help resolve or learned about someone's

5. Gallup®, CliftonStrengths® and the CliftonStrengths 34 Themes of Talent are trademarks of Gallup, Inc. All rights reserved.

goals and dreams in life that they want to achieve. Because you have laid foundational bricks in this relationship with the previous aspects of the BLESS model, you'll find people more accepting of and interested in the help you can offer. We can be prideful creatures sometimes, and we don't generally like to accept help from strangers. But the people we know and trust? We might turn to them for help before they even offer it.

Finally, we come to the *share* portion of BLESS. This last step is where, as a believer, you can look and pray for opportunities to share your relationship with Christ with them. Your personal experience with God can offer unique peace, wisdom, comfort, and insight to another person. You can tell stories of similar challenges and God's faithfulness that brought you through. You can compare the person's situation with a passage from the Bible to help them see that God is faithful to his promises. However, it is always good to gain permission before sharing. Sometimes, I'll say, "You know, what you're telling me reminds me of something I read in the Gospels the other day. Would it be okay if I shared this with you?" Most people are willing to allow me to share simply because I have built a trusted relationship with them. Remember, no one cares what you have to share until they know how much you care.

As you work through the BLESS model to develop strategies to love and serve different people in your life effectively, here are some helpful questions to sharpen your thinking:

1. If you could paint the perfect picture of your life at the end of this coaching process, what would it look like?

2. If God could paint a perfect picture through your life for the sake of blessing others, what would it look like?

3. What does it look like when those two pictures begin to merge together?

4. How does your Divine GPS begin to help you fill in the details as to your purpose in life?

5. Who needs what you uniquely have to offer in each of the areas of responsibility in your life (Church, Family, Lifework, and Society)?

6. What does your "why" begin to look like when you pull all three circles together?

There's a complete version of this questionnaire available at called2b.com/bless.

As you seek to make a difference, be on the lookout for making an impact in unexpected places or through unconventional methods. Ultimate frisbee, for example, is one of my favorite sports. I love tossing the disc back and forth with a good group, but I'd never thought of it as a way to share my faith, let alone love and serve others. When we lived in Singapore many years ago to help convince my mother-in-law to move back to the US with us, I got the chance to join a local ultimate frisbee league. It was a mix of local and expatriate players. The games became a great mix of competition and exercise as well as about finding a social circle to make some friendships. This ultimate frisbee group became extremely close, often sharing meals, going to the movies, or going out for drinks together.

As I got to know the people in this group, several months later, someone found out I was training to become a pastor. They jokingly asked, "Can pastors even play frisbee?" I said, "Yes, of course we can!" It was an incredibly diverse group—everything from atheists and agnostics to Buddhists, Muslims, and even a few disconnected Christians. If they had known I was a pastor-in-training from the start, many of them might have been more guarded or aloof. However, it was too late—they already liked me! Since we'd already cultivated relationships, we were able to keep playing and talk openly as a group. There were several different faiths and perspectives among us, but we were respectful, and it never became a barrier to our friendship.

A year later, tragedy struck. During one of our games, a massive storm rolled in, and a lightning bolt hit our field. One young man died from that lightning strike, and seven others were hospitalized.

The community we had created together was devastated; losing one of our own hit the entire group hard. It was during that time that many of them turned to me, looking for comfort and guidance. Thankfully, I was able to use my training as a pastor to help many of them process through the loss and find a sense of peace. But they did this because I was their friend first, not their pastor. In fact, if I had led with my religious title, I doubt any of them would have sought me out. They turned to me because we had cultivated a life and a trusted community together.

God worked through me during that time to help people I cared about get through a tragic event. Yet, I could easily have blown it if I hadn't followed the sequence of building community first. This experience from my past in Singapore is an example of where my Gifts, Passions, and Strengths intersected perfectly with people I directly influenced. As an added bonus, I was able to bless them with my knowledge and experience to help them find healing, emotionally and spiritually, during a difficult time.

As you look for the people and places that your calling fits into, remember to look where your hands can reach first. Always check first in your home, neighborhood, workplace, school, and church. Sometimes, that means just being in people's lives and building friendships. God has an incredible ability to pave the way and open the door for good things to happen. Your reach doesn't have to spread around the world to be effective. Just as trees do not have limbs that extend everywhere, so it is with you: wherever the tree sits, it is a sanctuary for those who need a place to rest in its shade.

13

Understanding Your Calling

How does it feel to have an understanding of your calling on this earth? By now, these three questions shouldn't feel so overwhelming:

- Who am I?
- Why am I here?
- What difference am I called to make?

Armed with answers, you can face the world with a sense of confidence in who you are and where you can make a difference. The old refrain "I don't know" or the vague definitions found primarily through your profession or relationships with others, you may now dismiss in peace. There's no need to continue languishing in a pit of confusion, uncertain of your direction and purpose. You've discovered your Gifts, Passions, and Strengths, the key ingredients in your unique identity. You have tangible words to help you express the best of who you are as a person. This Divine GPS can now guide you in your life journey.

Early on in my life journey, I grew up in a poor household. My parents grappled with (drug and alcohol) addictions, divorces, high stress, and a lack of resources. My family struggled to meet our financial obligations and often had difficulty paying for basic necessities like groceries. My parents fought constantly and didn't have the mental energy to pay attention to me between their day-to-day struggles and nightly disagreements.

I don't blame them under the circumstances. It isn't easy to be present with your family when you live so close to the edge. Survival mode stops us from making genuine connections or pursuing passions of any kind. The weight of worries like "How am I going to pay my rent?" or "How am I going to feed my kids?" makes enjoying life difficult. We didn't take vacations. To ponder how much more I could achieve in life was a foreign concept, and affirmation of any kind was in short supply.

I didn't know what my God-given talents were. No one ever helped me discover them. I never believed that I had gifts to offer the world. I didn't consider myself special or capable. In fact, in my eighth-grade year, I received three Fs, a C, and one A on my report card. (The A was from gym class because I could run really fast.)

I spent most of my childhood and teenage years in survival mode. Self-doubt poisons our minds and traps us in the orientation of our circumstances. Sometimes, even when we're aware we need to make a change, we still feel paralyzed. This rhythm of helplessness ruins our relationships and causes things we once loved to feel like burdens. It drains us of our passion. The echoes of these struggles continued to affect me during my years in college, as a young adult, and in ministry as a new pastor.

Deep personal searching occurred during my wilderness experience after my first pastoral call. In the presence of a strong and caring coach, God revealed the rescue he'd arranged for me. I stopped listening to my internal critic, partly because the coaching process forced me to go through multiple drafts to summarize my God-gifted identity. For the first time in my life, my identity rested squarely on who I am in Christ as a child of God. I had a clear understanding and articulation of what I was good at. I understood how I could impact the people around me in ways that engaged and made use of my God-given design. I understood my calling, where once I pondered whether I was even *worthy* of attempting great things, I now faced a different question: "*Will you answer the call?*"

I learned to ask a lot of new and different questions as well. Instead of asking, "Why me?" when I suffered, I began to ask, "Why not me?" When I ask it, I remember a well-known passage in the Bible where two of Jesus' apostles got into trouble with the religious authorities in Jerusalem. The book of Acts says that Peter and John, after an arrest, interrogation, and beating from the Sanhedrin, went off "rejoicing that they were counted worthy to suffer" for Christ (Acts 5:41 ESV). God can accomplish a *lot* through people who can look at suffering and pain objectively through a kingdom perspective.

I suppose I've come to see pain and suffering as part of the process of being called. Look at humanity's history, which is replete with people, including Christ himself, who refused to back away from pursuing their calling because it might be painful. The twelve disciples of Jesus, Martin Luther, Mother Teresa, Martin Luther King Jr.—all of these people dealt with significant pain and sorrow to benefit the world around them uniquely.

One of my favorite Bible passages is Rom 8:28 (NIV), in which the apostle Paul writes, "And we know that in all things God works for the good of those who love him, who have been called according to his purpose." The wonderful thing about God is that, in Christ, he doesn't just redeem us; he redeems all our hurts, pains, and mistakes and uses them for his glory. Growing up in Idaho, we have a different way of expressing Rom 8:28: "God makes flowers grow out of the manure of life." As a result, I can rejoice along with Paul in my suffering, knowing that "suffering produces endurance, and endurance produces character, and character produces hope, and hope does not put us to shame, because God's love has been poured into our hearts through the Holy Spirit who has been given to us" (Rom 5:3–5 ESV).

In the movie *50 First Dates*, Lucy Whitmore (played by Drew Barrymore) lives with a rare condition from a car accident: her memory resets every day. Every morning, she wakes up and forgets everything that happened the day before. Instead, Lucy thinks it's the day after her accident, which was also her father's birthday. She follows the same routine every day—goes to the same restaurant, paints the same painting, and makes the same plans to celebrate with her family. Her father and brother do their best to cope with the condition. They feel it's easiest to let Lucy think it's her father's birthday every day, and once she goes to sleep, they frantically re-set the house each night. Their small community on the island of Hawaii plays along, pretending that it's the same day before her car accident every day.

Lucy's tribe means well, but their methods keep her confined. Stuck in the same day every day, she misses out on new experiences. As the audience, we can easily imagine that, soon, Lucy will begin to show signs of age, as will her family and friends. It's no way to live a life, broken memories or otherwise.

Then, Henry Roth, played by Adam Sandler, comes along. Henry falls in love with Lucy, to the chagrin of her father and brother. They warn him not to get involved, believing it will worsen the problem. But Henry asks my favorite question: "Why not?"

Henry knows Lucy can be trusted with the truth. He believes she can handle finding out about the car crash and her memory loss each day as long as he reassures her that she is loved and shows her evidence that she loves him as well. Henry crafts a videotape for Lucy to watch each morning when she wakes up so she understands what happened, who she is, and how she ended up where she did. Because Henry asked, "Why not?" he created a path for them to live a full and healthy life together.[1]

I can't overstate the power of asking yourself, "Why not?" You'll have times when you puzzle over your purpose, or you'll be uncertain about exactly what to do. But imagine, for a moment, having that deep centeredness to retain your presence of mind when your identity and calling are challenged. Your calling is no longer smoke slipping through your fingers. It's tangible. Identifiable. Now, you have the power to live your life from the inside out instead of the outside in.

---

1. Peter Segal, dir., *50 First Dates*, Sony Pictures Entertainment, 2003.

Living life from the outside in is the default for many people. They rely on external sources to tell them who they are in life. This outside-in approach can mean using your job, accomplishments, or awards to define your identity. But putting such weight in these things eventually causes heartbreak. You will lose a competition or make a mistake at your job. Failure is imminent. It's a part of life, and it happens to everyone. If you rely on these things to define who you are, failure can feel catastrophic.

However, when we live life from the inside out, we consider who we are *first*. Our identity is the baseline of what we operate from. Through success and failure, we reinforce and understand who we are authentically. We can use this knowledge to our advantage by influencing outside factors with our Gifts, Passions, and Strengths. Even in some of the most challenging times, God can open doors for us. The only way you are able to navigate and step through those doors effectively is to know who you are and how you've been gifted.

By looking at your calling as your niche, which in business means producing content and products that align with your business goals and speak to a particular segment of the customer market, it makes you and your business unique. With a clearly defined niche, you are able to stand out against competitors and make consumers feel at home with your product. It is how products like Nike and Chanel make a brand that people want to define themselves by.

That is a lot like understanding your calling. You know what does and does not align with your goals. This clarity means you can more clearly blaze your path and have the opportunity to pursue things that align deeply with your values.

I hope the exercises and tools I've introduced to you throughout this book have helped you better understand your calling in life. In conclusion to the framework, I have developed the Called2B coaching dashboard. This coaching tool is a visual representation of the Called2B coaching process and serves as a compass to help navigate living out a believer's calling in Christ in love and service to one's neighbors.

14

Called2B Coaching Dashboard

LET'S REVISIT THE CALLED2B dashboard that we introduced earlier in the book. How do you now utilize this coaching tool to live out who you have been created and redeemed to be in love and service to your neighbor in your various callings in life?

Just like a GPS device for one's car or phone would be useless without maps loaded in, a believer's identity in Christ serves as a map for life, reminding them of who they are and what life is all about. The cross in the middle of the GPS symbol reminds us of our ultimate identity in Christ by grace through faith, which reminds us constantly of who we are and serves as a compass pointing to our true north, Jesus, as we live out our callings in everyday life. The GPS symbol reminds us of our unique identity of God's workmanship, gifting, and design in our lives (your Divine GPS). My hope is that this coaching dashboard will help you navigate life's callings and responsibilities with authenticity. The inner heart, soul, mind, and strength circle serves as a visual reminder, like a fuel gauge in a car, that we need to empower ourselves for life's journey. Finally, the outer circle represents the four domains, or areas of responsibility, of a believer's calling in their horizontal relationships with neighbors (people in our sphere of influence). This outer circle of Church, Family, Lifework, and Society also serves as a sort of gyroscope, reminding believers of the importance of keeping one's callings in life balanced.

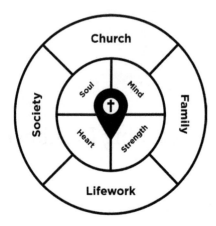

Called2B Coaching Dashboard

When you drive your car, your eyes continually watch for a few things. First and foremost, you observe that you are on the road. Then, you assess your gauges throughout the trip. You keep an eye on speed, gas, tire pressure, and oil because if any of these are empty, you won't make the trip safely. If you don't watch these gauges, you can cause irreparable damage to your vehicle. Your trip can come to a screeching and dangerous halt. And it will take some heavy lifting to get you back on track.

This Called2B coaching dashboard is a reminder to check those life gauges when it comes to living out your calling in Christ in your service to others in your daily callings. Put it where you will see it each day. Continually refer to it to ensure you are headed in the right direction. When you get busy, it is easy to lose focus. You can get pulled off course by many things. The death of a relative. The birth of a child. Medical procedures. Loss of a job. The list is endless. As significant events happen in our world, you may slightly turn away from the true north. In the beginning, you may only feel a little bit off. In fact, you may still have the original destination in your sights. But if you stay off true north long enough, you may end up in a completely different place over time.

Having this dashboard as a continual reminder can help us stay on track even when the unexpected happens. When it does, remember who you are at the core of your being. Remind yourself of your ultimate identity in Christ daily. Remember your Divine GPS and what empowers you. Living out your calling in life only works if you're aligned with your authentic identity. It's okay if you wander away for a while. It happens to the best of us. Life can be tricky and throw many distractions our way. When that happens, you now have the tools to course-correct. When you encounter stages where you need more comprehensive help, engage a coach. You don't have to navigate it alone.

15

A Journey of Transformation

THE FOLLOWING IS A story about a young man who had all that life could ever throw at him, and when he decided to pivot back to his true north, he sought out help. Jacob was a coaching client who was gracious enough to permit me to share his journey. In the early developmental stages of Called2B, he was one of the first participants coached in this process. I recently reconnected with him almost nine years later (at the time of writing) and learned how Called2B has helped him not only during life's struggles but even now, years later. Jacob's life is a far cry from the beginning when he and I first met.

At the time, Jacob felt lost. He was in the process of picking up the pieces of his life. Things were difficult for him right from the beginning. He battled a troubled childhood and drug addiction, and eventually faced jail time. He had just completed rehabilitation for his drug problem and was in a place of searching. He felt like an empty shell, hollowed out by the bad habits he had developed. He didn't know which way to turn or what to do next. He had no idea who he truly was in his life.

Mentally, before Called2B, I was newly sober and in recovery. I didn't know myself. With active addiction and substance abuse, you lose yourself. You don't know who you are. At that point in my life, I was grasping for anything to help me rediscover who I am.

His grandmother was a long-time member of the church I pastored, so Jacob did come to worship services every once in a while. He was trying to reconnect with his faith. He hoped God would help him understand the meaning and purpose of his life.

Recovery is hard. Some people have to go through it more than once. Jacob was going through the 12-step program a second time when he showed up to church on a weekend when, in my preaching, I shared about God's grace because of Jesus and described it as "undeserved love." After church that Sunday, Jacob joined a Bible study with some other young men he knew from recovery. As he drove home from that gathering, it hit him.

Jesus was there in that moment with Jacob as if he was sitting in the passenger seat. At that moment, he understood without a doubt who was his higher power. He felt peace for the first time in many years. This experience was his reconnection point. His soul felt peace, and he knew a loving God was watching him. The pathway to find his ultimate identity began to unfold.

In our personal journey of discovery, God wants us to discover things about him and learn things ourselves. He doesn't want to give us all the answers, like an encyclopedia. Jacob knew there was more he needed to understand about himself and who he was in Christ.

He continued to come to Sunday services during his search, and we got to know each other better. When I offered a coaching Empowerment Event with the Called2B framework to the congregation, he signed up quickly.

This Empowerment Event included many participants who wanted to learn about the principles of Called2B. After I took them through the one-day event, we invited participants to join a follow-up coaching triad for a deeper dive. This next step was the part where participants began to work closely with a coach. The triads consisted of three participants and a coach walking alongside.

In his triad, Jacob didn't feel like his mistakes defined him any longer. He was finally able to talk openly about the pain and trauma that led him to addiction. As many questions as Jacob had regarding life, those in his group asked many of the same questions he did. Each of them wanted to know who they were in Christ and what they were placed on earth to do. Together, they formed a small faith community, something Jacob had never experienced. That support was life-changing for him; he felt stable and secure. Getting together with other individuals who were willing to grow and learn was impactful for him. When discussing his experience, Jacob told us how he felt:

> I remember feeling . . . not so alone. Other people were struggling with decisions as well. We all wanted guidance on "what God wants for me." Those are the things that, up until that point in my life, I didn't have. I wasn't alone in looking for what God had in store for me.

When the time came to focus on their CliftonStrengths® results, Jacob's top five included Connectedness®, Ideation®, Developer®, Restorative™, and Individualization®.[1] Growing up, Jacob didn't receive much feedback about his natural talents, the best of who God created him to be in life. The people in his life focused mainly on the negative. It was eye-opening for him to see how God had uniquely gifted him. For the first time, he understood tangibly his God-given talents and had a clear definition of what those strengths meant and how they could impact others for good.

He felt invigorated to use them more.

Besides clarity on his unique identity and talents, CliftonStrengths® also helped Jacob recognize those things he was not as gifted at in life. He now understood that he was an idea man, but he needed support when it came to following through on his ideas. This "aha" discovery helped him realize that what he needed

---

1. Gallup®, CliftonStrengths® and the CliftonStrengths 34 Themes of Talent are trademarks of Gallup, Inc. All rights reserved.

in a life partner was someone who was strong on follow-through, like planning and organizing, so they could work together to bring these ideas to life.

Jacob's attitude was incredible. He was a sponge. I always tell people, "You get out of coaching what you put into it," and Jacob exemplified this. His goal was to start over and do things the right way. He showed up and worked hard. He was wholly invested in the process, and his enthusiasm helped create substantive, meaningful change in his life.

As he discovered his strengths, I told Jacob his homework was to go back and talk to the people who knew him best. The goal was to see if the assessment results truly reflected who he was and what they saw in him. This exercise, I've found, is more effective than asking people who only know us at a surface level. We're prone to wonder if they truly see us, especially if they haven't seen us at our best or worst. We'll wonder whether they're telling us the truth of what they see in us. So Jacob's task was to talk to people who *did* know him at his core. He had to ask them what they thought about his assessment results and whether they recognized those traits in him. It's more powerful to have confirmation from someone you love, especially if they've helped you through your darkest times. Jacob's closest family and friends had endured plenty of his darkest days, and they confirmed his results wholeheartedly.

Now, Jacob could point to the evidence of his results through the affirmation of others and not doubt them. He could highlight his strengths in job interviews. We coached him on how to answer interview questions about his rehab and jail time. This experience gave him a safe place to practice answering difficult questions about his past while his group acted as a sounding board for how he could respond. He could be bold and confident about what and how he could add to an organization while still being humble and honest about his failures if they entered the discussion.

Through coaching, Jacob worked to discern what direction he should take regarding his career. He narrowed it down to a pair of opportunities: an apprenticeship as an electrician or a restaurant management position. Both roles contained opportunities for advancement, and both also featured duties and responsibilities that were either pros or cons for him. He learned how to articulate his strengths, even if he hadn't necessarily developed or utilized them before. He learned constructive ways to address his weaknesses. The goal was to help him *stand through* the negative instead of running away from it, to leverage it, and to demonstrate how he had *grown* in his character from his experiences.

Jacob eventually landed the restaurant management position, which became the first of many steps for him in a highly fulfilling career. He loved his work as a manager, especially when he got to coach the young people he worked with on a daily basis. Usually, they were fresh out of high school, or they needed a job and took a minimum wage position. Jacob's knowledge and experience with discovering his strengths empowered him to help others he worked with grow. He loved the fulfillment that came from developing others and passing on what he'd learned.

As the story continued, Jacob found his first employer didn't have an interest in promoting him further, nor did they value the coaching development he offered. When some people get stuck in situations like these, they either resign or go to *resignation*, working in what some call a dead-end job. But Jacob understood that his values made it clear he was no longer aligned with the position. He was working seventy to eighty hours a week, managing three different locations, and sacrificing time with his family and kids. He wanted to work for a company that appreciated his strengths and didn't ask so much of him.

So, he quit.

In a recent conversation, Jacob shared that he would *never* have done that before. He had always been financially motivated when it came to a job. But this wasn't the same old Jacob. Without any new job lined up or knowing his next move, he followed his Divine GPS. Jacob felt good about this time of transition because he knew who he was and wanted something more out of life. The fulfillment he felt when helping others was so satisfying he was willing to take a pay cut to find a job where helping others was valued.

This crucial decision is where God stepped in for Jacob. His mother-in-law used to work for the State Department of Health and Welfare as a peer support specialist. At the time, she wanted to transition out of her role. She told him about the job and how it involved helping the less fortunate. It was a coaching role where he could work with people fighting mental illness and addiction. He could support people and work directly with them to help improve their lives.

Jacob interviewed for the job and landed the position quickly. It is a job he relishes and looks forward to doing every day because it aligns with his passion for helping people through life's struggles, as he had experienced. He feels fulfilled and continues to make a significant impact in the lives he encounters on a daily basis.

What's more, he is *good* at his job. Jacob is now a key employee in the organization, where his manager often leans on him to care for the well-being of his coworkers. It's an intense and stressful job. Workers deal with overdoses, suicide, relapses, broken relationships, and destructive behaviors, which can wear on even the healthiest of souls. With his past experience, Jacob can talk people through their thoughts and worries. He helps them see things from the addict's perspective, which is often confounding and counter-productive. His coworkers have a better understanding of their clients' frame of mind so that they can serve them better.

Jacob is making a difference. More importantly, *he knows* he's making a kingdom impact. *"I thought you are supposed to just go on with life, and it didn't matter what you were good at,"* he initially said. *"Instead, you have to seize the opportunities available and put up with it."*

Today, Jacob feels joyful and fulfilled in his work. His job was custom-designed for someone with his Gifts, Passions, and Strengths, so he gets one chance after another to help his neighbor in this new role each day. His Divine GPS keeps him on the right path. Through the Called2B coaching process, Jacob went from being under the influence to being a person of influence.

> *I get so many blessings in my life from the people I work with today. I'm going into people's homes where they are*

still actively using [drugs], and I get to help them and be where they are at and be that hand of God. I'm fortunate to do what I do.

Called2B also went beyond helping Jacob in his work life. In our interview, he told us about his relationship with his kids and how he wouldn't have been able to communicate with them without the guiding hand of the Called2B principles. He is able to joke with them, and they sincerely desire his presence in their lives. They connect deeply as a family and love each other. Jacob is grateful that by understanding who he was created to be for the sake of being a blessing to others, he can help his kids understand who they are at their core. His wife was drawn to the passion and strengths he discovered through Called2B. She has learned to offer her own strengths to help him make good on his ideas.

"I don't think I have ever felt more comfortable with who I am since learning those things and applying them in my life," Jacob said. He described his experience with the Called2B coaching experience as "transformational." However, the coaching framework was only 50 percent of the equation; he had to put in the hard work of applying what he learned about himself. He took the time to learn about himself and who God created and redeemed him to be. He made a point of studying how he could make the most impact in the world around him. Then, with God's grace and blessing, he put the plan into action.

The Called2B coaching framework can be transformative for your life, too. But just like Jacob, *you have to make the investment* and look to your Divine GPS for guidance. Be committed to change, be willing to work on yourself, and seek fulfillment. When you look for places where you can make an impact based on God's design and gifting, you'll be amazed at how your life will change and how *you* will change the lives of others in the process.

16

What Now?

YOUR LIFE HAS ENORMOUS significance. You are meant to do meaningful, impactful things. Your calling is God-given, and it is intended to bless others and bring glory to God. The work you do with your gifting is important. You have a holy calling to make a unique impact in the lives of others through your Divine GPS. I'm grateful you allowed me to take you on this journey. You should feel a healthy sense of accomplishment, having looked inward and outward to discover who you have been called to be.

Where you might have been unsure of who you are and the road you were supposed to take, you now know your God-given gifts and strengths. Not only that, you now understand your core motivations in the form of your passions, and you have a path for how you can make an impact in the world around you. Perhaps, when you first started reading, you were in a time of transition. Or, maybe you needed guidance to experience life to the fullest. In either case, know that living from your *authentic identity* in Christ will move you closer and closer to being fulfilled.

Both your *ultimate identity* as well as your *unique identity* will fill you with confidence in a new setting. They will ground you.

When things fall apart around you, or you experience tragedy, you will be able to stand on who *you* are created and redeemed to be. Our circumstances may change, but who we are at our core, especially who we are in Christ, stays consistent. You are now equipped to weather the storms of life.

So, where do you go from here?

Implementing these changes will be challenging on your own. It's easy to get discouraged, fall back into old habits, or take the easy way out. To live our calling in Christ to its fullest, we need to be content in any circumstance, whether we're doing well or otherwise. Living aligned to your Divine GPS takes intentionality, especially if you've identified significant changes to make in your life. I encourage you to find someone who can help you stay on the right path—someone to walk alongside you, who cares for and encourages you, who truly listens to you and asks the right questions.

I'm talking about a coach.

Coaches serve to help you find answers that make sense for who you are and your context rather than tell you what to do with your life. As a coach, I walk alongside those I work with like we would on a hiking trail and help you discover potential destinations, as well as help you identify upcoming obstacles that could get in the way of achieving your goals. Your coach might say, "Hey, there's a boulder in the way; how are you going to get around it?" or "There is a stream in your way; how are you going to cross over it?" A coach is supposed to help you navigate and overcome challenging terrain as you reach your destination. A coach enables you to stay on track.

Too often, we have a tendency to think that if we follow the map of a successful person, we, too, will find gold. Surely, you can see, especially after the pandemic, that many of the maps that *used* to work no longer do. They're like trying to read a map for Seattle to find our way around New York City. Everyone is confused, trying to find their ultimate destination. It's rare to meet anyone who has it all figured out. However, a coach is like having a compass to aid you. I can help you find your "true north" by asking powerful questions. These questions turn your gaze inward to discover an inexhaustible source of genuine strength flowing from your authentic identity in Christ, intended for service in God's kingdom. As you go forward in life, you can be confident that you're on the right path, even when you don't know what lies ahead.

A coach helps empower you to live out your callings in life. I don't want you to be like me or follow the steps I have taken. I want to help you to be *you*! I want you to understand your true north, your ultimate identity in Christ, and what you uniquely offer to the world according to your unique identity. I want to help you remember, as you journey through life, how important it is to care for yourself so you can be empowered to love and serve your neighbor more effectively in all of your areas of responsibility in life.

As an International Coaching Federation (ICF) trained professional certified coach (PCC) and Gallup®-certified Strengths coach, I've helped people do this for over two decades. I've seen hundreds of people make positive changes in their lives. Many of them were young people, especially with an entrepreneurial spirit. Together, we have worked to discern their identity, purpose, gifts, and their unique pathways to live lives of impact in love and service to others.

So where can you find me?

First, check out the Called2B podcast. On this show, we interview guests who offer valuable insight and personal experience with the Called2B coaching framework. It's a great way to help you understand and remember who you have been called to be in your daily life. Listen in as you are heading to work in your car, working on chores at home, or relaxing on a day off. In each podcast, we discuss how you can implement this kingdom framework of calling in your life. Our guests are fantastic people who share a wealth of experience. I think you'll enjoy the conversation!

Second, you can check out our website, Called2B.com. There, you can schedule a discovery meeting with me to find out if coaching is right for you. We'll discuss your goals and coaching options. I also would love to hear your thoughts on this book! The secret sauce of change and transformation truly emerges through working together with a trained and certified professional coach.

Whether it's another coach you work with or me, I encourage you to find someone who serves as your confidential creative think partner. Eventually, I am also looking to develop an e-learning platform and subscription newsletter so you can get Called2B content delivered to your inbox every week.

Lastly, through my website, you can schedule a Called2B Empowerment Event with me. This in-person or online gathering is where we build the team that helps bring forth your identity and calling in Christ. It could be your family, friends, coworkers, or members of your church. We'll work through the Called2B elements and help you discern your unique calling, individually and collectively. You'll deepen your awareness of your purpose and grow together through group or team coaching. Do you remember the story of Jacob, the young man I coached? It was the Empowerment Event that became the first step in his journey of transformation.

Even if you aren't ready to do anything right now, I hope that you have still learned a *lot* from simply reading this book. You may want to take the information you've learned and try it out on your own. There is nothing wrong with that. It's far better than doing nothing!

One thing I recommend along the way is to check in with your Called2B coaching dashboard. In our world today, we've never had such quick access to so many voices, so much information, and such a plethora of alternative narratives to live by. It's easy to forget the principles you've learned, so check in with yourself periodically. Revisit the goals you created here and review your Divine GPS during some daily downtime. Remember your "why" when things get difficult. Most of all, by regularly revisiting your goals, you can recognize when you have wandered away from God's calling on your life in service to others.

I created an acronym to help you identify when you're drifting. It's called "MOODS." The letters stand for five clear emotional and energetic symptoms that, like pain signals in the body, are meant to warn us that something's wrong:

- M—Monotony
- O—Overworked
- O—Overwhelmed
- D—Disengaged
- S—Self-Focused

When I stray from living a life aligned with my Divine GPS, I get into one of those moods. That's why the acronym MOODS is so helpful; a mood swing is like a keyword search on Google that triggers me to remember the acronym. If I don't feel like myself, or if I don't want to go anywhere or do anything, I'm usually slipping back into my former self. Or perhaps I feel lethargic, and things seem much more challenging than they should be. It can be a sign I've become concerned with how I can serve myself instead of how to serve others. That's how it feels when you stray from your divine purpose. *Monotony* creeps in, you feel stuck in a rut, and things no longer excite or interest you. It's time for some kingdom perspective!

Feelings of being *overworked* are next. You're doing too much for others without taking enough time to care for your wellness and well-being. Remember, when we're trying to make an impact in the four stations of life, it doesn't mean you work until you drop! Establishing a healthy rhythm of self-care is essential and a key to success. Between too much work and stressful events like family trauma or loss, sudden unemployment, or even the birth of a child, we become *overwhelmed*. We forget who we are and the goals we've set for ourselves because we are so concentrated on the implications of these big shifts in our lives.

If we continue to ignore the signs, we'll begin to feel *disengaged*. Now, we're struggling to live in the present moment. It's hard to pay attention to your family or enjoy a fun event when you're preoccupied with things beyond your control. It leads us to the bottom of the barrel, where we become *self-focused*. At this point, we no longer ask how we can help others; our only concern becomes how we might make things easier for ourselves. Times of self-focus are when we begin to have a pity party, and no one wants to attend one of those!

Does this sound familiar, especially in our modern Western lifestyles? If you feel these symptoms, it's a good bet you're straying from your authentic identity in Christ. However, don't be too hard on yourself. Straying from your calling can happen for many reasons. Honestly? It *will* happen. It happens in my life all the time. That's why I felt the need to write this book, so you can recognize when you are off track and course-correct. If we ignore these signs and disregard our calling, we'll end up in a state of anxiety, depression, confusion, or cynicism, much like when I wandered in the wilderness and couldn't be the man my family needed me to be. I felt lost and uncertain. We are still susceptible to the pitfalls and uncertainties of life on this side of eternity.

When you feel pain, your brain is telling you something is wrong. When you experience MOODS, that's your soul telling you the same thing. Listen to those messages, and ask yourself, "What is causing them? What changes or adjustments do I need to make?" Come back to the lessons and exercises you completed in this book. Compare your actions with the goals and plans you made for impact. How well are you doing? Where have you fallen back into old ways?

Then, it's time to course-correct. Recenter your focus. Look at the four stations of life and ask, "Where can I get back on track?" Most of all, give yourself grace, just as Jesus gives it to you every day as his new creation. You're headed somewhere *intentional*. This book is for people who want to live life on purpose; it won't work if you think life is a random, undirected series of unrelated events. You took the time to learn about who you are and your divine calling, and you're taking the steps you need to make to be a greater blessing to others around you. You are a child of God, created in his likeness to serve others and make a significant kingdom impact in their life.

As you continue on your journey, let's recap the options for how you can take part with Called2B:

What Now?

1. Do you want to soak it all in before you take a step? Check out the Called2B podcast.

2. Do you want to dive in deeper and learn more? Check out the Called2B.com website for more resources and updates.

3. Do you believe you're ready to partner with someone on the journey and want to dive into coaching? Book an online discovery meeting with me!

Thank you for your time, interest, and willingness to explore the unknown. Believe that you are put in this place at this time for a specific purpose. I fully believe God wants to do significant things throughout your life to bless those around you, and I'm eager to see how you put your Divine GPS into action. I will leave you with my favorite scripture for encouragement for those times when I am unsure of what to do next:

> "For I know the plans I have for you," declares the LORD, "plans to prosper you and not to harm you, plans to give you a hope and a future." (Jer 29:11 NIV)

May God's richest blessings be upon you!

Printed in the USA
CPSIA information can be obtained
at www.ICGtesting.com
JSHW050047300924
70609JS00003B/11

9 798385 208210